Library of
Davidson College

**Internal migration
in developing countries**

Internal migration in developing countries

A review of theory, evidence, methodology and research priorities

Michael P. Todaro

Published with the financial assistance of the
United Nations Fund for Population Activities

International Labour Office Geneva

301.32
T 633i

Copyright © International Labour Organisation 1976

Publications of the International Labour Office enjoy copyright under Protocol 2 of the Universal Copyright Convention. Nevertheless, short excerpts from them may be reproduced without authorisation, on condition that the source is indicated. For rights of reproduction or translation, application should be made to the Editorial and Translation Branch, International Labour Office, CH-1211 Geneva 22, Switzerland. The International Labour Office welcomes such applications.

ISBN 92-2-101598-X (limp cover)
ISBN 92-2-101599-8 (hard cover)

First published 1976
Second impression 1980

The designations employed in ILO publications, which are in conformity with United Nations practice, and the presentation of material therein do not imply the expression of any opinion whatsoever on the part of the International Labour Office concerning the legal status of any country or territory or of its authorities, or concerning the delimitation of its frontiers.
The responsibility for opinions expressed in signed articles, studies and other contributions rests solely with their authors, and publication does not constitute an endorsement by the International Labour Office of the opinions expressed in them.
ILO publications can be obtained through major booksellers or ILO local offices in many countries, or direct from ILO Publications, International Labour Office, CH-1211 Geneva 22, Switzerland. A catalogue or list of new publications will be sent free of charge from the above address.

Printed by Imprimerie La Concorde, Epalinges, Switzerland

83-7736

CONTENTS

Introduction 1

1. **Urban surplus labour : dimensions of a global problem** 7
   Urbanisation and migration 7
   Urban labour force growth : past and projected 10
   Magnitude and age structure of urban unemployment 11
   Linkages between urban surplus labour, poverty and income distribution 14

2. **In search of a "general" framework for migration analysis** 15
   Ravenstein's "laws" of migration 15
   Lee's theory of migration 16
   A critique of Lee's theory 19

3. **Economics of internal migration in developing countries : a review of models** 21
   The Lewis-Fei-Ranis model of development 21
   Towards an empirically testable "economic" model of internal migration 25
      The migration process 26
      Migrant characteristics 27
      An economic theory of rural-urban migration 28
         The basic nature of the Todaro migration model 28
         A mathematical formulation 32
         Modifications of the basic Todaro model 36
         Conclusions 45

4. **Converting theoretical migration models into econometric equations : a review of alternative methodological approaches** 47
   The econometric migration function : "micro" versus "macro" estimation 47
      "Micro" function estimation 48
      "Macro" function estimation 50
   Common variables used in both micro and macro econometric migration studies 51
   Census versus survey approaches : strengths and weaknesses 53

Choosing between different sample survey approaches: fitting objectives with methodology 56
Problems of measuring variables in migration functions 57
    Measuring migration 57
    Measuring rural incomes 58
    Measuring urban incomes: actual and expected 59
A final note on econometric estimation techniques and simulation . . . 60
    Econometric estimation 60
    Simulation 62

5. Summary review of quantitative migration studies 65

Summary results of the non-rigorous descriptive literature 65
    Who migrates? 65
    Why do people migrate? 66
    What are the economic effects of migration on source and destination areas? 66
Survey of recent econometric migration literature 67
    Importance of income and employment differentials 68
    Importance of job probabilities and urban unemployment rates . . . 69
    Urban employment expansion, wage differentials, job probabilities and induced migration 70
        Job expansion and induced migration 70
        Wage differentials and induced migration 71
        Conclusions 72
    Differential responsiveness of population subgroups and the effects of personal contacts and distance 72
    Private economic benefits of migration 73
        Private returns 74
        Education and income 74

6. Looking towards the future: priorities for migration research 75

Migration and development: a list of research priorities 75

7. Some final observations 81

Appendices 83

A. Selected migration functions 83
B. Some illustrative rough estimates of "threshold" migration elasticity coefficients with respect to urban job creation, selected developing countries, 1970 88
C. A simple proof of the "threshold" urban job elasticity formulae of equations (14) and (15) 90

Bibliography 91

INTRODUCTION

As recently as a decade ago, internal migration in general and rural-urban migration in particular were receiving favourable comment in the economic development literature. Rapid internal migration was thought to be a desirable process in which surplus rural labour was gradually withdrawn from traditional agriculture to provide cheap manpower to fuel a growing modern industrial complex (Lewis, 1954; Fei and Ranis, 1961).[1] The process was deemed socially beneficial (at least on the basis of historical evidence — Kuznets, 1964 and 1971) since human resources were being shifted from locations where their social marginal products were often assumed to be zero to places where this marginal product was not only positive but also rapidly growing as a result of capital accumulation and technological progress.

Herrick (1965) reflected the prevailing view about the desirability of internal migration when he asserted that "In the absence of any movement, when rural fertility exceeds urban fertility, [...] the agricultural labour force will grow faster than industrial employment. Movement from the countryside to the towns, necessary if strictly balanced growth of the two parts of the labour force is to occur, becomes even more imperative if an increase in the size of the industrial sector is among the goals of the developing economy." Only a few years later, however, Jolly (1970) seemed to be reflecting a changing attitude among economists towards the question of migration when he noted that "Far from being concerned with measures to stem the flow, the major interests of these economists [i.e. those who stressed the importance of labour transfer] was with policies that would *release* labour to *increase* the flow. Indeed, one of the reasons given for trying to increase productivity in the agricultural sector was to release sufficient labour for urban industrialisation. How irrelevant most of this concern looks today!"

---

[1] For bibliographical details, see pp. 91 ff.

Internal migration in developing countries

Numerous studies have now documented the fact that, throughout the developing world, rates of rural-urban migration continue to exceed rates of urban job creation and to surpass greatly the capacity of both industry and urban social services to absorb this labour effectively. No longer is rapid migration viewed by economists as an unambiguous beneficient process necessary to solve problems of growing urban labour demand. On the contrary, *migration today is being increasingly looked upon as the major contributing factor to the ubiquitous phenomenon of urban surplus labour and as a force which continues to exacerbate already serious urban unemployment problems caused by growing economic and structural imbalances between urban and rural areas.*

Migration exacerbates these rural-urban structural imbalances in two major direct ways. First, on the supply side, internal migration disproportionately increases the growth rate of urban jobseekers relative to urban population growth, which itself is at historically unprecedented levels, because of the high proportions of well educated young people who dominate the migrant stream. Their presence tends to swell the growth of urban labour supply while depleting the rural countryside of valuable human capital. Second, on the demand side, most urban job creation is more difficult and costly to accomplish than rural employment creation because of the need for substantial complementary resource inputs for most modern sector industrial jobs. For example, an ILO estimate of investment costs per worker in Egypt in 1969 showed a cost of US$5,070 for an industrial job compared with US$616 for an agricultural job (ILO, 1969). Moreover, the pressures of rising urban wages and compulsory fringe benefits for employees, in combination with the unavailability of "appropriate" (i.e. usually more labour-intensive) production technologies, mean that a rising share of output growth in the modern sector is accounted for by increases in labour productivity. Together this rapid supply increase and lagging demand growth tend to convert a short-run problem of manpower imbalances into a long-run situation of chronic and rising urban surplus labour.

But the impact of migration on the development process is much more pervasive than its obvious accentuation of urban unemployment and underemployment. In fact, the significance of the migration phenomenon in most developing countries is not necessarily in the process itself or even in its impact on the sectoral allocation of human resources. It is in the context of its implications for economic growth in general and for the "character" of that growth, particularly its distributional manifestations, that migration research has assumed growing importance in recent years.

We must recognise at the outset, therefore, that migration substantially in excess of new job opportunities is both a symptom of and a contributing factor to underdevelopment in the Third World. An understanding of the causes, determinants and consequences of internal migration is thus central to a better understanding of the nature and character of the development process and to the formulation of appropriate policies to influence this process in socially desirable ways. A simple yet crucial step in emphasising the central position of the migration phenomenon is to recognise that *any economic and social policy that affects rural and urban real incomes will directly and/or indirectly influence the migration process. This process in turn will itself tend to alter the pattern of sectoral and geographic economic activity, income distribution and even population growth.*

Since all economic policies have direct and indirect effects on the level and growth of either urban or rural incomes or both, they all will have a tendency to influence the nature and magnitude of the migration stream. Although some policies may have a more direct and immediate impact (e.g. wages and income policies, programmes of employment promotion, etc.), there are many others which, though less obvious, may in the long run be no less important. These policies would include, for example, alterations in the system of land tenure, commodity pricing, rural credit allocation, taxation, export promotion, import substitution, commercial and exchange rate policies, the geographical distribution of social services, the nature of public investment programmes, attitudes towards private foreign investors, the organisation of population and family planning programmes, the structure, content and orientation of the educational system, the structure and functioning of urban labour markets, and the nature of public policies towards international technological transfer and the spatial allocation of new industries. There is thus a clear need to recognise the central importance of internal migration and to integrate the two-way relationship between migration and population distribution, on the one hand, and economic variables, on the other, into a more comprehensive analytical framework designed to improve development policy.

In addition, we need to understand better not only why people move and what factors are most important in their decision to move but also what are the consequences of internal migration for rural and urban economic and social development. If all development policies affect and are affected by migration, which are the most significant and why? What are the policy options and trade-offs among different and sometimes competing objectives (e.g. curtailing internal migration and expanding educational opportunities in rural areas)? In short, unless we can begin to quantify the relative impact of different economic policies on the nature, character and magnitude of such migration and to ascertain what factors influence a person's decision to move in different countries and regions, we shall be unable to formulate policies to deal effectively with the dual problems of rapid urban population growth and rising urban marginalism.

Our broad objectives in this book are fourfold: first, to examine carefully the literature on migration models and the role of internal migration in the process of economic development; second, to identify what has been empirically tested and where, giving special emphasis to a number of recent econometric country studies; third, to explore the strengths and limitations of various methodological approaches to estimating the parameters of micro- and macro-econometric migration functions based on both census and survey data, and to suggest the most promising avenues for further investigation; and fourth, building on these foundations, to identify the major priority questions in migration research which still remain to be answered and to suggest appropriate methodological approaches for dealing with them.

To this end the book is divided into seven chapters. Chapter 1 surveys the dimensions of the problem of urbanisation and urban surplus labour in developing nations. Chapters 2 to 5 review and analyse the alternative theoretical, empirical and methodological approaches to migration research. In Chapter 2 we briefly review the main strands of the more general descriptive literature on internal migration, stressing both "non-economic" and economic approaches. Chapter 3 provides a summary of recent theoretical trends in the literature on economic migration, focusing on extensions and modifications of the basic Todaro "expected income" model of rural-urban migration. Chapter 4 analyses various methodologies for converting theoretical migration models into testable econometric equations. Here we look at alternative specifications of micro and macro migration functions, the strengths and limitations of census versus survey approaches to data generation, problems of measuring variables, and the pros and cons of different econometric estimation techniques. In Chapter 5 we ask the question "What do we think we now know about the migration process?" A survey of both the empirical descriptive literature on migration and particularly the new econometric literature provides the basic information for answering this central question.

Finally, in Chapters 6 and 7 we try to identify the priority issues for future migration research and suggest ways in which a carefully focused world-wide research programme might contribute substantially to the advancement of our understanding of the nature of the migration process and its relationship to population growth and economic development. In particular, it is argued that by increasing the policy content of future migration studies we shall be better able to assist Third World governments to formulate appropriate economic strategies designed to influence the magnitude and pattern of internal migration in more socially desirable ways.

Introduction

The author is at present Visiting Professor of Economics at the University of California, Santa Barbara, United States. An earlier version of this book was prepared as background material for the International Labour Office's newly initiated research project on migration and employment. Comments by T. Paul Schultz, G. Rodgers and J. Mouly are greatly appreciated.

URBAN SURPLUS LABOUR: DIMENSIONS OF A GLOBAL PROBLEM

1

URBANISATION AND MIGRATION

Much has been written about the extraordinary growth of world population over the past few decades.[1] Almost 75 per cent of that growth has occurred in developing countries. By 1976 the world's population had passed the 4,000 million mark, and projections for the year 2000 indicate a range of anything between 6,000 and 9,000 million people (ILO, 1974, table 3A). But, whatever the figure eventually reached, one thing is clear: nowhere will population growth be more dramatic than in the major cities of the developing world. In the second half of this century the number of people living in cities and towns throughout the world as a whole will double. But in the Third World, unless effective remedial measures are adopted soon, urban population will more than quadruple as rural peasants and educated youths flood into the cities in search of increasingly elusive, and in many cases non-existent, modern sector jobs.

Current rates of urban population growth range from under 1 per cent per annum in two of the world's largest cities, New York and London, to 6 to 7 per cent in most African countries, with Asian and Latin American cities growing at annual rates of 4 to 6 per cent. As table 1 dramatically illustrates, the world's 12 fastest growing cities are all located in developing nations. Each of these cities is expected to double in size over the 15-year period from 1970 to 1985. Some, such as Bandung, Lagos and Karachi, are projected to increase even more substantially during this short period than have any cities in history over a similar span. The major source of this urban growth, however, will *not* be natural population increase. Rather it will be the continuing in-migration of rural people. Over 50 per cent of urban growth in many developing nations is due to the accelerated pace of rural-urban migration (see table 2). The way in which governments in developing countries plan to

---

[1] For two excellent summary reviews see Berelson (1974) and ILO (1974).

Internal migration in developing countries

Table 1. The world's fastest growing cities

City	1970 population (in millions)	1985 projected population (in millions)	Over-all growth rate (percentage)
Bandung (Indonesia)	1.2	4.1	242
Lagos (Nigeria)	1.4	4.0	186
Karachi (Pakistan)	3.5	9.2	163
Bogotá (Colombia)	2.6	6.4	146
Baghdad (Iraq)	2.0	4.9	145
Bangkok (Thailand)	3.0	7.1	137
Teheran (Iran)	3.4	7.9	132
Seoul (Republic of Korea)	4.6	10.3	124
Lima (Peru)	2.8	6.2	121
São Paulo (Brazil)	7.8	16.8	115
Mexico City (Mexico)	8.4	17.9	113
Bombay (India)	5.8	12.1	109

Source: International Planned Parenthood Federation (1974), p. 10.

Table 2. Growth and concentration of urban population in eight countries

Country	Urban population as percentage of total population		Average annual population growth rate			Percentage of urban population born elsewhere	
	Year	Percentage	Period	Percentage		Year	Percentage
				Total	Urban		
Mexico							
Urban places (2,500 people and over)	1970	59	1960-70	3.3	4.8	1970	22
			1950-60	3.1	4.9		
25 largest cities (100,000 people and over in 1970)	1970	37	1960-70		4.9	1970	29
			1950-60		4.9		
Mexico City metropolitan area (8.6 million people in 1970)	1970	18	1960-70		5.1	1970	37
			1950-60		5.1		
Brazil							
Urban places (administrative definition)	1970	56	1960-70	2.8	5.0	1970	40
			1950-60	3.2	5.5		
Rio de Janeiro (4.3 million people in 1970)	1970	5	1960-70		2.8	1970	42
São Paulo (5.2 million in 1970)	1970	6	1960-70		5.1		
Ghana							
Towns (5,000 people and over)	1970	29	1960-70	2.4	4.8	1960	70+
			1948-60	3.6	9.2		
Accra (0.6 million people in 1970)	1970	7	1960-70		5.0		
Adults (15 years and over) only			1948-60		8.2		

Table 2 (continued)

Country	Urban population as percentage of total population		Average annual population growth rate			Percentage of urban population born elsewhere	
	Year	Percentage	Period	Percentage		Year	Percentage
				Total	Urban		
Tanzania							
Urban places (administrative definition)	1967	6					
Largest towns (19,000 people and over in 1971)	1967	4	1967-71	n.a.	4.7	1971	84+
			1948-67	2.5	6.8		
Dar es Salaam (0.3 million people in 1971)	1967	2	1967-71		3.3	1971	84+
Adults only			1948-67		7.5		
Kenya							
Urban places (2,000 people and over)	1969	10	1962-69	3.4	7.1		
Nairobi (0.5 million people in 1969)	1969	5	1962-69		15.2 [1]	1969	76
Republic of Korea							
32 urban places (50,000 people and over)	1970	41	1960-70	2.3	5.5	1970	50
Seoul (5.5 million people in 1970)	1970	18	1960-70		7.8	1970	57
India							
Urban places (5,000 people and over)	1971	20	1961-71	2.2	3.3	1961	39
			1951-61	2.0	2.7		
Metropolitan areas (100,000 people and over)	1971	10	1961-71		4.1		
			1951-61		4.0		
Calcutta	1971	1	1961-71		2.0		
Bombay	1971	1	1961-71		3.7		
Pakistan							
Urban places (5,000 people and over)	1972	26	1961-72	3.6	4.8		
Metropolitan areas (500,000 people and over)	1972	10	1961-72		4.9		

[1] African population only. n.a. = not available.
Source: Yap (1975), table 1.

cope economically, politically and socially with such phenomenal urban population growth will be a crucial ingredient in the success or failure of their long-term development strategies.

Although the rapid growth of urban populations in developing countries is a ubiquitous phenomenon, there still exist considerable variations in urban concentration and growth across countries. Table 2 shows the proportion of the total population living in urban areas as well as the urban growth rates for eight countries. They have been compiled primarily from 1970 census sources but take account of a number of modifications by individual researchers for different countries (Yap, 1975, table 1). Two measures of urban location are provided in the table : *(a)* all urban areas, as defined by the census ; and *(b)* a fixed number of larger cities, reported either individually or as a group. Clearly, the first measure is very sensitive to the definition of "urban", which can vary from one country to the next and from one census to the next. It thus has a tendency to exaggerate urban growth rates between census years as a result of the addition of more urban places and alterations in urban boundaries. As Yap correctly points out, the second measure does not have this bias and at the same time has the advantage of focusing on the larger cities where the problems of poverty and in-migration are the most serious.

But whatever measure is used, urban growth resulting from rapid migration has been substantial. For most developing nations migration accounted for anything between 40 and 65 per cent of urban population increase between 1960 and 1970. Since many migrants are unmarried jobseekers, the proportion of urban labour force growth resulting from migration during this same period is even larger. Finally, in terms of the migration status of the urban population, we see from the last column of table 2 that the proportion of persons born outside the city can be as high as 57 per cent in Seoul (Republic of Korea), 76 per cent in Nairobi (Kenya) and over 84 per cent in Dar es Salaam (Tanzania).

URBAN LABOUR FORCE GROWTH: PAST AND PROJECTED

The number of people searching for work in a less developed country depends primarily on the size and age composition of its population. The processes relating trends in over-all population growth to the growth of indigenous labour forces take on numerous forms. Two are of particular interest, however (Stolnitz, 1974). First, whatever the over-all magnitude of the population growth rate, its fertility and mortality components have a *separate* significance. A natural growth rate of 3 per cent (or 30 per 1,000) when crude birth and death rates are 50 and 20 per cent has implications for the labour force that are different from those when the birth and death rates are 40 and 10 per cent. This is because the age structure of the population will be different for an economy with a high birth and death rate than for one with a low birth and death rate, even though the natural rate of increase is the same for both. Since birth rates obviously affect only the numbers of newly born while death rates tend to affect (albeit unevenly) all age-groups, in a high birth and death rate economy a greater percentage of the total population will fall into the age-dependent (i.e. 1-15 year) group than in a low birth and death rate economy. This result is mitigated, however, to the extent that death rates in developing countries remain heavily influenced by infant mortality. The rapid reductions in death rates recently experienced by most developing countries, therefore, have on balance contributed to an expansion of the size of their present labour forces while continuous high birth rates create high present dependency ratios and rapidly expanding future labour forces.

Second, the impact of fertility declines on labour force size and age structures is felt only after very long lags, even when these declines are rapid. The reason is the well-known phenomenon of population "momentum" widely referred to in the demographic literature (see, for example, Berelson, 1974). For example, a sudden halving of developing countries' fertility rates by the late 1970s would reduce the male labour force by only 13 per cent by the end of the century — a reduction from about 1,270 million to 1,110 million workers. This reduction is certainly not trivial and its long-run impact would clearly be substantial. Nevertheless, the essential fact remains that over the next 15 years those who enter the labour force have already been born, while the size of the labour force over the next 25 years is fairly well determined by current fertility and mortality rates.

Present labour force projections suggest annual increases of the order of 2.1 per cent for all less developed regions during the present decade, and approximately 2.4 per cent and 2.6-2.8 per cent for the 1980s and 1990s respectively (see table 3). But within the Third World, Latin American countries are likely to experience the greatest rates of labour force growth over the next 25 years while Asian and African countries follow close behind. In terms of actual numbers, however, which bring out the prospective magnitude of the developing countries' employment problem more dramatically than do rates of growth, reasonable projections for the year 2000 indicate that there will be over 920 million new jobseekers more than in 1970, with over 45 per cent of these in south Asia and 31 per cent in east Asia (see table 4). Unless viable and productive economic opportunities can be created in rural areas, a sizeable proportion of these people will be forced to seek work in the already congested urban localities.

MAGNITUDE AND AGE STRUCTURE OF URBAN UNEMPLOYMENT

Given high rates of urban labour force growth in the range of 4 to 7 per cent per annum and the relatively slower growth of urban employment opportunities (averaging about 2.5 per cent), the problem of urban surplus labour has attained very serious proportions in many developing countries. Current

Internal migration in developing countries

Table 3. Projected annual rates of labour force growth, 1970-2000 (percentage)

Country category or region	Labour force growth rate		
	1970-80	1980-90	1990-2000
Category			
Developed countries	1.1	0.9	0.9
Less developed countries	2.1	2.4	2.6-2.8
Region			
South Asia	2.3	2.6	2.9
East Asia	1.6	2.1	2.5
Africa	2.2	2.5	2.7
Latin America	2.8	3.0	3.3

Source: ILO (1974), table 8.

Table 4. Labour force projections, 1970-2000 (in millions and as percentage of total)

Country category or region	Size of labour force							
	1970		1980		1990		2000	
	Millions	%	Millions	%	Millions	%	Millions	%
Category								
Developed countries	488	32.5	542	30.4	593	27.6	649	25.1
Less developed countries	1 012	67.5	1 239	69.6	1 547	72.4	1 933	74.9
Region								
South Asia	429	42.3	537	43.2	691	44.5	886	45.6
East Asia	376	37.1	440	35.4	519	33.4	602	31.0
Africa	132	13.1	165	13.3	212	13.7	277	14.3
Latin America	74	7.3	97	7.8	129	8.3	172	8.9

Source: ILO (1974), table 3A.

rates of open unemployment (i.e. relating to people without any regular or part-time jobs) in the cities of Africa, Asia and Latin America average about 10 to 15 per cent of the urban labour force, or approximately 34 to 51 million people. But the problem is considerably more serious for those between the ages of 15 and 24, many of whom have had significant amounts of schooling. Table 5 shows that, in almost all urban centres in developing countries, the rates of unemployment in this age bracket are almost double the rates of recorded unemployment for the urban labour force as a whole.

Urban surplus labour: a global problem

Table 5. Rates of urban unemployment by age, in selected years (percentage)

Country	Area	Year	Age 15-24 years	15 years and above
Africa				
Ghana	Large towns	1960	21.9	11.6
America				
Argentina	Buenos Aires	1965	6.3 [1]	4.2 [2]
Chile	Urban areas	1968	12	6 [3]
Colombia	Bogotá	1968	23.1	13.6
Curaçao		1966	37.7	18.8
Panama	Urban areas	1963/64	17.9 [4]	10.4
Uruguay	Mainly urban areas	1963	18.5	11.8
Venezuela	Urban areas	1969	14.8	7.9
Asia				
India	Urban areas	1961/62	8.0	3.2 [5]
Iran	Teheran City	1966	9.4	4.6
Rep. of Korea	Non-farm households	1966	16.3	8.9
Malaysia	Urban areas	1965	21.0	9.8
Philippines	Urban areas	1965	20.6 [6]	11.6 [7]
Singapore		1966	15.7 [4]	9.2
Sri Lanka	Urban areas	1968	39.0	15.0
Thailand	Bangkok	1966	7.7	3.4

[1] 14-29 years.   [2] 14 years and above.   [3] 12 years and above.   [4] 15-29 years.   [5] 15-60 years.
[6] 10-24 years.   [7] 10 years and above.
Source: from Turnham (1971), table III.2.

Rates of "open" urban unemployment, however, only reveal the *visible* aspects of the employment problem in Third World nations, the tip of an enormous iceberg. The actual underutilisation of labour takes many other forms, including various manifestations of underemployment and hidden unemployment (Edwards, 1974, pp. 10-12). Although data on the various forms of underemployment in Third World cities are scarce, the reports of recent ILO comprehensive employment strategy missions to Colombia, Kenya, the Philippines and Sri Lanka indicate that as much as 30 per cent of the population — over 100 million people — in Third World urban areas may be considered to be greatly underutilised (for further estimates, see Sabolo, 1975, table 3).

LINKAGES BETWEEN URBAN SURPLUS LABOUR, POVERTY AND INCOME DISTRIBUTION

There is an important relationship between migration, high levels of urban unemployment and underemployment, widespread poverty and unequal distributions of income. For the most part, those without regular urban employment or with only scattered part-time employment are also among the very poor. Those who do have regular paid employment in the public and private sectors are typically among the middle- to upper-income groups. But it would be incorrect simply to assume that everyone who does not have an urban job is necessarily poor, while those who work full time are relatively well off. This is because there may be many unemployed urban workers who are "voluntarily" unemployed in the sense that they are searching for a specific type of job, perhaps because of high expectations based on their presumed educational or skill qualifications. They may refuse to accept jobs which they feel to be inferior and are able to do this because they have outside sources of financial support (e.g. relatives, friends, local money-lenders). Such people are unemployed by definition, but they may not be poor.

Similarly, there are many individuals who may work full time in terms of hours per day but may, nevertheless, have very little income. Many self-employed and petty wage workers in the so-called urban "informal" sector (e.g. traders, hawkers, craftsmen, taxi drivers, petty service providers, workers in repair shops, etc.) may be so classified. Such people are by (Western) definition fully employed but often they are still very poor.[1]

In spite of the above reservations about a too literal linkage between unemployment and poverty, it still remains true that one of the major mechanisms for reducing poverty and inequality in developing countries is the provision of adequate paying productive employment opportunities for the very poor. Clearly, the mere creation of more employment opportunities in urban areas should not be considered as the sole, nor even perhaps as the major, solution to the urban poverty problem. Such a solution requires much more far-reaching economic and social measures focused primarily on rural areas (Todaro, 1969). But the provision of more work and the wider sharing of the work that is available would go a long way towards reaching that goal. Employment creation, therefore, must be an essential ingredient in any development strategy directed at reducing poverty. The important issue for our purposes, however, relates to the optimal spatial distribution of any new employment opportunities and how these influence internal migratory patterns.

---

[1] See ILO (1972), Ch. 13, for an extensive discussion of economic life in the urban informal sector of Kenya (note that Leys (1973) considers that the picture painted is perhaps rather idealised). Hart (1974) also provides an interesting analysis of urban informal sector activities in Ghana.

IN SEARCH OF A "GENERAL" FRAMEWORK FOR MIGRATION ANALYSIS 2

RAVENSTEIN'S "LAWS" OF MIGRATION

Everett S. Lee, the sociologist, has provided what is probably the most appealing and most concise "general", non-rigorous framework for analysing the internal migration process (Lee, 1966). Lee begins his discussion by noting that many of the generalisations or "laws" of migration developed by E. G. Ravenstein in his two classic papers (Ravenstein, 1885 and 1889) have stood the test of time and still remain starting-points for much contemporary migration theory. Ravenstein's "laws" of migration may be summarised in the form of six basic propositions:

(1) Migration and distance. The rate of migration between two points will be inversely related to the distance between these points. Migrants who travel long distances will tend to "go by preference to one of the great centres of commerce and industry" (Ravenstein, 1885, p. 199).

(2) Migration by stages. There will normally be "currents of migration" in which a country's inhabitants tend to move first towards nearby towns and eventually gravitate towards the most rapidly growing cities.

(3) Stream and counterstream. "Each main current of migration produces a compensating counter-current" (Ravenstein, 1885, p. 199). While rural-urban migration may dominate the over-all "current" or stream of migration there will always be a counterstream of reverse urban-rural migration so that "net" migration from point i to point j will always be less than "gross" migration between these two points.

(4) Urban-rural differences in propensities to migrate. "The natives of towns are less migratory than those of the rural parts of the country" (Ravenstein, 1885, p. 199). Thus "net" internal migration streams will normally have a rural-urban predominance.

(5) Technology, communications and migration. Migration streams will have a built-in tendency to increase over time as a result of increases "in the

means of locomotion" and a "development of manufactures and commerce" (Ravenstein, 1889, p. 288).

(6) Finally, and most important, dominance of the economic motive. "Bad or oppressive laws, heavy taxation, an unattractive climate, uncongenial social surroundings, and even compulsion (slave trade, transportation), all have produced and are still producing currents of migration, but none of these currents can compare in volume with that which arises from the desire inherent in most men to 'better' themselves in material respects" (Ravenstein, 1889, p. 286). In short, the economic motive is always predominant in the matrix of factors influencing the decision to migrate.

Writing in the mid-1960s, Lee makes the following observation in his review of Ravenstein's migration analysis.

In the three-quarters of a century which have passed, Ravenstein has been much quoted and occasionally challenged. But, while there have been literally thousands of migration studies in the meantime, *few additional generalisations have been advanced* (Todaro's italics). True, there have been studies of age and migration, sex and migration, race and migration, distance and migration, education and migration, the labour force and migration, and so forth; but most studies which focused upon the characteristics of migrants have been conducted with little reference to the volume of migration, and *few studies have considered the reasons for migration* (Todaro's italics) or the assimilation of the migrant at destination (Lee, 1966, p. 48).

Much has changed in the ten years since Lee wrote this paragraph. The principal reason for this sudden change has been the heightened interest of a growing number of younger, better-trained economists in the field of migration studies (especially with respect to migration within and from developing countries). As we shall see below, the appearance of new theoretical models of migration and new "generalisations" about the migration process in the development literature, combined with the growing proficiency of economists in survey research methodologies, data analysis and econometric techniques, has produced a steadily increasing volume of new insights. More important, for the first time it has permitted careful quantification of the importance of different variables influencing the decision to migrate, at both the micro and the macro levels. It has therefore opened up the field for the exploration of alternative policies designed to influence migration in more socially desirable ways. We shall return to this new phenomenon later.

LEE'S THEORY OF MIGRATION

In his paper, Lee attempts to develop a general schematic framework for analysing the volume of migration, the development of "streams" and "counterstreams" and the characteristics of migrants. He begins with a broad definition of migration simply as "a permanent or semi-permanent change of

Figure 1. Origin and destination factors and intervening obstacles in migration

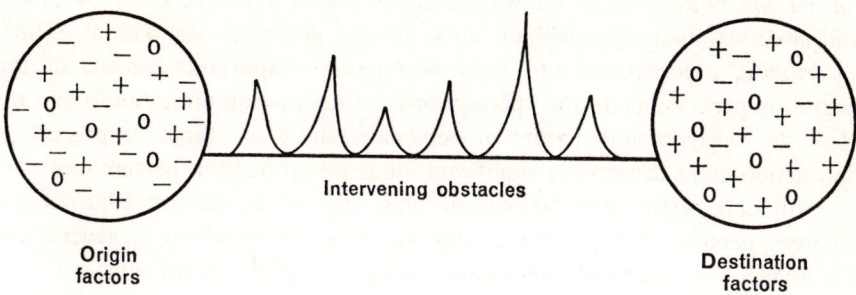

Source: Lee (1966), p. 50.

residence" and goes on to note that "no matter how short or how long, how easy or how difficult, every act of migration involves an origin, a destination, and an intervening set of obstacles" (Lee, 1966, p. 49).

The factors which enter the decision to migrate and the migration process can therefore be summarised under four general categories:

(1) Factors associated with the area of origin.
(2) Factors associated with the area of destination.
(3) Intervening obstacles.
(4) Personal factors.

Lee then provides a useful schematic diagram, reproduced above as figure 1, to illustrate the first three of the above four categories. Every origin and destination area is assumed to have positive forces (the "pluses" in figure 1) which hold people within the area or "pull" others to it; negative forces (the "minuses" in figure 1) which repel or "push" people from the area; or zero forces (the "zeros" in figure 1) which on balance exert neither an attractive nor a repellent force and towards which people are therefore essentially indifferent. The effect of each of these forces will vary with the personality as well as the other individual traits (e.g. age, education, skill level, sex, race, ethnic or tribal group, etc.) of different people.

The sets of $+$, 0 and $-$ may therefore be defined differently at both origin and source for different individuals: i.e. one man's plus (e.g. a good educational training programme) may be another's zero (e.g. someone who already possesses that level of education) or even negative factor (e.g. as a result of local school taxes levied on all residents of the area). But, by and large, there exist general sets of factors towards which most people tend to react in the same way (higher wages, more job opportunities, better amenities, etc.). What is important is the ability to identify these factors and to quantify their influences on different classes of people. One significant difference between origin and destination factors, however, is that people living in the former will possess better knowledge of the precise outcome of origin pluses and minuses than they will of those in the potential destination. Thus, *uncertainty*, *expectations* and *risks* become an important element in the migration process, as do the "perceptions" of destination pluses and minuses. Here the existence and nature of personal, family or ethnic "contacts" in destination areas can exert a significant influence on migrant perceptions.

Although origin and destination plus and minus factors adjusted for different personality traits go a long way towards providing a general explanation of internal and international migration, they are not sufficient. Lee therefore introduces the concept of "intervening obstacles" set between all origin and destination points. Some intervening obstacles may provide only minor friction (distance, transport costs, etc.) while others may be insurmountable (restrictive immigration laws, quotas by race or national origin, physical controls over population movements). As in the case of origin and destination pluses and minuses, intervening obstacles will tend to exert differing influences on different people. What may be a minor obstacle to one potential migrant (e.g. the transport cost of moving for a financially well off individual) may be a major obstacle to another (e.g. the same transport cost to a very poor person).

Lee then utilises his basic conceptualisation of migration as involving a set of origin and destination factors, a set of intervening obstacles and a series of personal factors to formulate a number of general hypotheses about the volume of migration, the development of stream and counterstream and the characteristics of migrants. A sample of the most important of these hypotheses is summarised below (Lee, 1966, pp. 53-57).

Volume of migration
(1) The volume of migration within a given territory varies *directly* with the degree of diversity of areas included in that territory.
(2) The volume of migration varies *directly* with the diversity of people.
(3) The volume of migration is *inversely* related to the difficulty of surmounting the intervening obstacles.
(4) Unless severe checks are imposed, both the volume and the rate of migration tend to increase with time.

Stream and counterstream
(5) Migration tends to take place largely within well defined streams (e.g. from a variety of rural regions to regional towns and then towards the major cities).
(6) For every major migration stream, a counterstream develops (i.e. there will always be return migrants who find that their initial perceptions did not accord with reality or who simply failed to achieve their objectives).
(7) The magnitude of the "net" stream (i.e. stream minus counterstream) will be directly related to the preponderance of minus factors at origin — i.e. origin "push" factors are relatively more important than destination "pull" factors.

Characteristics of migrants
- (8) Migration is selective, i.e. migrants are not random samples of the population at the origin.
- (9) Migrants responding primarily to plus factors at destination tend to be "positively" selected, i.e. they are of a higher "quality" (more educated, healthier, more ambitious, etc.) than the origin population at large.
- (10) Migrants responding primarily to minus factors at origin tend to be "negatively" selected, e.g. most European migrants to North America in the nineteenth and early twentieth century were unskilled rural peasants driven off the land by economic hardship, political and/or religious persecution, etc.
- (11) The degree of "positive" selection increases with the difficulty of the intervening variables, i.e. the more educated are willing to travel longer distances to find suitable employment opportunities.

A CRITIQUE OF LEE'S THEORY

While Lee's general theory of migration summarised above is appealing because of its simplicity and persuasive because of the intuitive validity of many of its hypotheses, it is of limited help for policy analysis in developing countries because of its high degree of generality and the interdependence of many of its hypotheses. More important, the apparent validity of many of the hypotheses does not lead us to determine which plus factors and which minus factors at both origin and destination are quantitatively the most important to different groups and classes of people. Nor does the existence of intervening obstacles help us to know which are major and which are minor. Moreover, the theory provides no insights into possible "trade-offs" between plus and minus factors nor the range of possible migration responses to alternatives in the magnitude and/or the sign of plus and minus factors. In short, by not specifying the inter-relationships between dependent and independent variables within the context of a rigorous theoretical framework, Lee's theory of migration and, indeed, most other "non-economic" social science migration models offer little practical policy guidance for decision-makers in developing nations.

In seeking such practical policy guidance we must inevitably turn to the economist's formulation of the migration problem and to econometric methods for evaluating the quantitative significance of alternative explanatory variables. Although the rigorous economic literature on migration in developing countries is a phenomenon of the very recent past, it is a potent literature with important new theoretical insights into the migration process and the beginnings of a carefully documented, econometric specification and quantification of the most important determinants of internal migration in a small but growing number of Third World countries.

ECONOMICS OF INTERNAL MIGRATION IN DEVELOPING COUNTRIES: A REVIEW OF MODELS

3

THE LEWIS-FEI-RANIS MODEL OF DEVELOPMENT

The first, and most well known, model of development to give consideration, at least implicitly, to the process of rural-urban labour transfer was that developed by Sir W. Arthur Lewis (Lewis, 1954) and later formalised and extended by John Fei and Gustav Ranis (Fei and Ranis, 1961). The Lewis-Fei-Ranis (L-F-R) model became the received "general" theory of the development process in "labour surplus" Third World nations during most of the late 1950s and 1960s. In the L-F-R model the economy consists of two sectors: *(a)* a traditional, *rural subsistence sector* characterised by zero or very low productivity "surplus" labour; and *(b)* a high productivity modern *urban industrial sector* into which labour from the subsistence sector is gradually transferred. The primary focus of the model is both on the process of labour transfer and on the growth of employment in the modern sector. Both labour transfer and urban employment growth are brought about by output expansion in the modern sector. The speed with which they occur is given by the rate of industrial capital accumulation in the modern sector. Such investment is made possible by the excess of modern sector profits over wages on the assumption that "capitalists" reinvest all of their profits. Finally, the level of wages in the urban industrial sector is assumed to be constant and determined as a fixed premium over a constant subsistence level of wages in the traditional agricultural sector (Lewis assumed that urban wages would have to be at least 30 per cent higher than average rural income to induce workers to migrate from their home areas). However, at the constant urban wage, the supply of rural labour was considered to be perfectly elastic.

Let us examine a simple illustration of the L-F-R model. In figure 2 the process of modern sector growth is depicted. On the vertical axis we have the real wage and the marginal product of labour (assumed to be equalised in the competitive modern sector) and on the horizontal axis the quantity of labour.

Figure 2. The Lewis-Fei-Ranis model of growth and employment in a dual labour-surplus economy: the modern sector

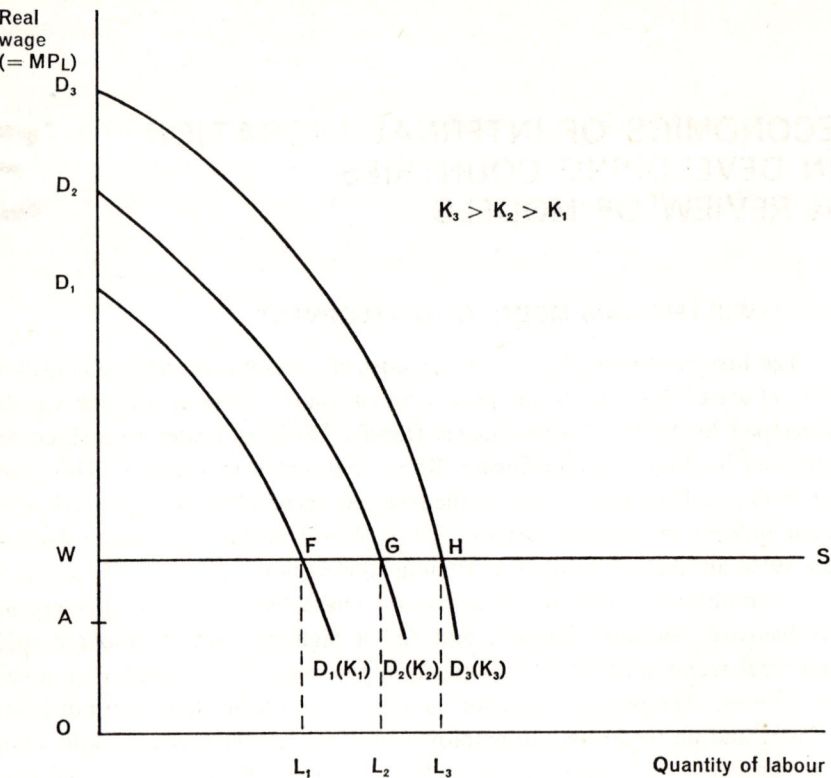

OA represents the average level of real subsistence income in the traditional rural sector. OW, therefore, is the real wage in the capitalist sector. At this wage the supply of rural labour is assumed to be "unlimited" or perfectly elastic, as shown by the horizontal labour supply curve WS. Given a fixed supply of capital, K_1, in the initial stage of modern sector growth, the demand curve for labour is determined by labour's declining marginal product and is shown by curve $D_1(K_1)$. Since profit-maximising modern sector employers are assumed to hire labourers up to the point where their marginal physical product is equal to the real wage (i.e. the point F of intersection between the labour demand and supply curves), total modern sector employment will be equal to OL_1. Total modern sector output would be given by the area bounded by points OD_1FL_1. The share of this total output which is paid to workers in the form of wages would be equal, therefore, to the area of the rectangle $OWFL_1$. The surplus output shown by the area WD_1F would be the total profits that accrue to the capitalists. Since it is assumed that all these profits are reinvested, the total capital stock in the modern sector will rise from K_1 to K_2. This larger capital stock causes the total product curve of the modern sector to rise, which in turn induces a rise in the marginal product or demand curve for labour. This outward shift in the labour demand curve is shown by line $D_2(K_2)$ in the figure. A new equilibrium urban employment level will be established at point G with OL_2 workers now employed. Total output rises to OD_2GL_2 while total wages and profits increase to $OWGL_2$ and WD_2G respectively. Once again, these larger (WD_2G) profits are reinvested, thus increasing the total capital stock to K_3, shifting the labour demand curve to $D_3(K_3)$ and raising the level of modern sector employment to L_3.

The above process of modern sector growth and employment expansion is assumed to continue until all "surplus" rural labour is absorbed in the urban industrial sector. Thereafter the labour supply curve becomes positively sloped and both urban wages and employment will continue to grow. The structural transformation of the economy will have taken place with the balance of economic activity shifting from rural agriculture to urban industry.

Although the L-F-R model of development is both simple and roughly in conformity with the historical experience of economic growth in the West, it makes three key assumptions which are at variance with the realities of migration and underdevelopment in most contemporary Third World countries.

First, the model implicitly assumes that the rate of labour transfer and employment creation in the urban sector is proportional to the rate of urban capital accumulation. The faster the rate of capital accumulation, the higher the growth rate of the modern sector and the faster the rate of new job creation. But what if surplus capitalist profits are reinvested in more sophisticated labour-saving capital equipment rather than just duplicating the existing capital, as is implicitly assumed in the L-F-R model? Figure 3 reproduces the basic model; however, this time the labour demand curves do not shift uniformly outward but, in fact, cross. Demand curve $D_2(K_2)$ has a greater negative slope than $D_2(K_1)$ to reflect the fact that additions to the capital stock embody labour-saving technical progress.

We see that even though total output has grown substantially (i.e. OD_2EL_1 is significantly more than OD_1EL_1), total wages ($OWEL_1$) and employment (OL_1) remain unchanged. All the extra output accrues to capitalists in the form of excess profits. Figure 3, therefore, provides an illustration of what some might call "anti-developmental" economic growth, i.e. *all* the extra income and output growth is distributed to the few owners of capital while the

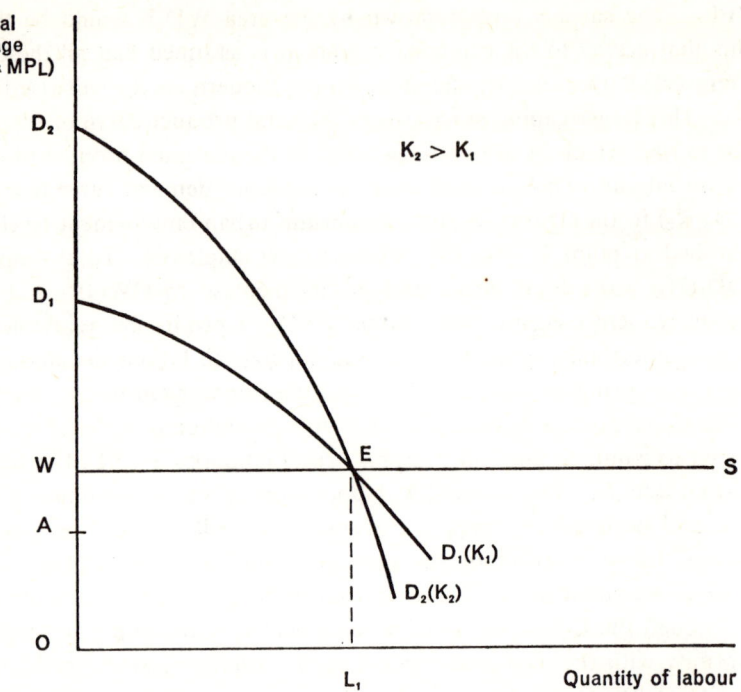

Figure 3. Labour-saving capital accumulation destroys the employment implications of the Lewis-Fei-Ranis model

income levels of the masses of workers remain largely unchanged.[1] Even though total GNP would rise, a poverty-weighted index of development (see Chenery, Duloy and Jolly, 1973, Ch. 3) would show no improvement in aggregate social welfare.

The second key (but questionable) assumption of the model is that "surplus" labour exists in rural areas while there is full employment in the urban areas. Most contemporary research indicates that the reverse may be true in many Third World countries, i.e. there is substantial open unemployment and underemployment in urban areas but little general surplus labour in rural locations, especially during planting and harvesting periods. True, there are exceptions to this rule (e.g. parts of the Asian subcontinent and isolated regions of Latin America where land ownership is very unequal); but, by and

---

[1] Although one could provide a counter-argument that in the long run these rapidly rising capitalist profits and capital-intensive production methods will generate even higher rates of output growth and thus provide for the eventual rise in living standards for all (Galenson and Leibenstein, 1955), the experience of many developing countries is that capitalists often do *not* save and reinvest their profits in socially productive ways but may instead devote them to conspicuous consumption or transfer them overseas (Ranis, 1962; Gupta, 1970).

large, many development economists seem to agree that the assumption of urban surplus labour is becoming empirically more valid than the opposite L-F-R assumption of general rural surplus labour (see, for example, Edwards, 1974, Chs. 1 and 2; Sabot, 1975b; Turnham, 1971).[1]

The third key assumption at variance with reality is the notion of the continued existence of constant real urban wages until the point where the supply of rural surplus labour is exhausted. One of the most striking features of urban labour markets and wage determination in almost all developing countries has been the tendency for these wages to rise substantially over time, both in absolute terms and relative to average rural incomes, even in the presence of rising levels of open unemployment.

We may conclude therefore that, when one takes into account the labour-saving bias of most modern technological transfer, the limited existence of rural surplus labour, the growing prevalence of "urban surplus" labour and the tendency for institutionally determined urban wages to rise rapidly even where substantial urban open unemployment exists, the L-F-R model offers limited analytical and policy guidance for understanding Third World employment and migration problems. Our remarks, however, are not intended to minimise the historic and analytical importance of the L-F-R model or to overlook the fact that it does emphasise two major elements of the employment problem: the structural and economic differences between the rural and the urban sectors, and the central importance of the process of labour transfer which links them together. With these two elements in mind, we may now turn to some of the more contemporary and widely utilised models of rural-urban migration and urban unemployment in developing countries.

TOWARDS AN EMPIRICALLY TESTABLE "ECONOMIC" MODEL OF INTERNAL MIGRATION

Until recently, research on internal migration in developing countries has been dominated largely by the work of geographers, demographers and sociologists. For the most part, economists have preferred to ignore problems of internal migration and unemployment while operating within the confines of traditional neoclassical two-sector models, with their automatic price adjustment mechanisms, allocative efficiency assumptions and full employment implications. And yet a better understanding of the causes and determinants

---

[1] On the "impossibility of rural surplus labour" under reasonable assumptions concerning strict risk aversion on the part of peasant families, see Hamilton (1975). Sen (1966) had developed the necessary and sufficient condition (i.e. a constancy of the marginal rate of substitution between income and effort) for the existence of rural surplus labour in a celebrated earlier article.

Internal migration in developing countries

of rural-urban migration and the relationship between migration and relative economic opportunities in both urban and rural areas is central to any analysis of Third World employment problems. Government policies to ameliorate the urban unemployment problem must be based, in the first instance, on a knowledge of the migration process, particularly who comes to town and why.

The migration process

The factors influencing the decision to migrate are varied and complex. Since migration is a *selective process* affecting individuals with certain economic, social, educational and demographic characteristics, the relative influence of economic and non-economic factors may vary not only between nations and regions but also within defined geographical areas and populations. As pointed out above, much of the early research on migration tended to focus on social, cultural and psychological factors while recognising but not carefully evaluating or quantifying the importance of economic variables. Emphasis has been placed, for example, on the following influences.

(1) Social factors, including the desire of migrants to break away from the traditional constraints of inhibiting rural social structures.

(2) Physical factors, including climatic and meteorological disasters such as floods, droughts and famine which force people to seek alternative living environments.

(3) Demographic factors, including the reduction in mortality rates and the concomitant high rates of rural population growth leading to rapidly rising rural population densities.

(4) Cultural factors, including the existence of urban "extended family" relationships which provide initial financial security to new migrants and the attraction of the so-called "bright city lights".

(5) Communication factors, resulting from improved transportation, urban-oriented educational systems and the "modernising" impact of the introduction of radio, television and the cinema, all of which modify the impact of Lee's "intervening obstacles".

Needless to say, all these mostly "non-economic" influences are relevant. However, there now seems to be widespread agreement among economists and non-economists alike that migration can be explained primarily by the influence of economic factors. These economic factors include not only the standard "push" from stagnating subsistence agriculture and the "pull" of relatively high urban wages, but also the potential "push-back" (Lee's "counterstream") of high urban unemployment.

Migrant characteristics

It is convenient to divide the main characteristics of migrants into three broad categories: demographic, educational, and economic.

(1) Demographic characteristics. The principal demographic characteristic of urban migrants in Third World countries is that they tend mostly to be young, single males between the ages of 15 and 25. Various studies in Africa and Asia have provided quantitative evidence of this phenomenon (see, for example, Caldwell, 1969; Byerlee, 1974; Brigg, 1971; Yap, 1975; and Connell *et al.*, 1975). However, the proportion of migrating women also seems to be on the increase as their educational opportunities expand. For example, in Latin America the growing literature on migration indicates that women apparently are now in the majority of the migration stream, largely as a result of Latin America's relatively advanced state of urbanisation as compared with other developing areas (Brigg, 1971; Nelson, 1974; Connell *et al.*, 1975).

(2) Educational characteristics. One of the most consistent findings of rural-urban migration studies is the positive correlation between educational attainment and migration (see the references above). There seems to be a clear association between the level of completed education and the propensity to migrate, i.e. those with more years of schooling, everything else being equal, are more likely to migrate than those with fewer years. For example, in a recent study of Tanzania by Barnum and Sabot (1975) the positive relationship between levels of education and propensity to migrate is very clearly documented for the period 1955 to 1970. Moreover, the impact of declining urban employment opportunities on the educational characteristics of the more recent migrants was revealed to be quite significant. Tanzanian secondary school leavers were found to constitute a rising proportion of the migration stream while those with only a primary education showed a much slower increase. This phenomenon can be attributed to the fact that limited urban employment opportunities were being "rationed" by educational levels and only those workers with some secondary education had a decent chance of finding a job (Edwards and Todaro, 1973). Those with only a primary school education or less found it very difficult to secure regular urban employment. Their proportionate numbers in Tanzania's "migrant stream" therefore, have begun to decline.

(3) Economic characteristics. It is very difficult to make any valid generalisations about the economic characteristics of migrants. For many years the largest percentage of internal migrants were those poor, landless, unskilled individuals whose rural opportunities were for the most part

non-existent. In colonial Africa seasonal migration was a dominant factor with migrants from various income levels seeking short-term urban jobs (Caldwell, 1969; Gugler, 1968). Recently, however, with the emergence of a stabilised, modern industrial sector in most urban areas, the financial assets of migrants from rural areas have assumed greater importance, at least to the extent that individuals with larger financial resources can survive longer while searching for the elusive urban job. Thus, rural migrants appear to come from two major economic classes (Lipton, 1976): *(a)* very poor, landless and illiterate peasants who are predominantly "pushed" into towns or towards other rural areas; and *(b)* relatively well off, better educated workers who are more likely to be "pulled" into larger towns by attractive economic opportunities. However, in practice it is very difficult to separate push from pull factors. Within these two economic groups the relatively poor rural migrants still predominate in the over-all stream in absolute terms, if only because the greater percentage of rural inhabitants are relatively poor.

An economic theory of rural-urban migration

As we have seen, the evidence of the 1960s in which many developing nations witnessed a substantial migration of their rural populations into urban areas in spite of rising levels of urban unemployment and underemployment calls into question the validity of a number of traditional models of labour transfer and economic development. In a series of articles the author and others have attempted to fill this gap in migration theory by developing a model of rural-urban migration which attempts to explain the apparently paradoxical relationship (at least in terms of traditional neoclassical economics) of accelerated rural-urban migration in the context of rising urban unemployment.[1] We therefore examine the nature of the basic Todaro model and some of its variants.

The basic nature of the Todaro migration model

Starting from the assumption that migration is based primarily on privately rational economic calculations for the individual migrant despite the existence of high urban unemployment, the Todaro model postulates that migration proceeds in response to urban-rural differences in *expected rather than actual earnings*. The fundamental premise is that migrants as decision-makers consider the various labour market opportunities available to them as between,

---

[1] See, for example, Todaro (1968, 1969, 1971b and 1976a); and Harris and Todaro (1970).

say, the rural and the urban sectors, and choose the one which maximises their "expected" gains from migration. Expected gains are measured by *(a)* the *difference in real incomes between rural and urban job opportunities* and *(b)* the *probability of a new migrant obtaining an urban job*. A schematic framework describing the multiplicity of factors affecting the decision to migrate is given in figure 4. While the factors illustrated in figure 4 include both economic and non-economic variables, the economic ones are assumed to predominate.

The "thought process" of the Todaro model can be explained as follows. Suppose the average unskilled or semi-skilled rural worker has a choice between being a farm labourer (or working his own land) for an annual average real income of, say, 50 units per year, or migrating to the city where a worker with his skill or educational background can obtain wage employment yielding an annual real income of, say, 100 units. The more traditional economic models of migration, which place exclusive emphasis on the income differential factor as the determinant of the decision to migrate, would indicate a clear choice in this situation. The worker should seek the higher paying urban job. It is important to recognise, however, that these migration models were developed largely in the context of advanced industrial economies and, as such, implicitly assumed the existence of full employment or near-full employment in urban areas. In a full employment environment the decision to migrate can in fact be predicated solely on securing the highest paying job wherever it becomes available, other factors being held constant. Simple economic theory would then indicate that such migration should lead to a reduction in wage differentials through geographical changes in supply and demand, both in areas of out-migration (where incomes rise) and in points of in-migration (where they fall).

Unfortunately, such an analysis is not very realistic in the context of the institutional and economic framework of most Third World nations. First of all, these countries are beset, as we have seen, by a chronic and serious problem of urban surplus labour with the result that many migrants cannot expect to secure a high paying urban job immediately upon arrival. In fact, it is much more likely that upon entering the urban labour market many migrants will either become totally unemployed or will seek casual and part-time employment in the urban traditional sector for some time.[1]

Consequently, in his decision to migrate the individual must in effect balance the probabilities and risks of being unemployed or underemployed for a considerable period against the positive differential between urban and rural

---

[1] For an empirical verification of this hypothesis see, among other studies, Hay (1974), table 4.7, for Tunisia; and Carvajal and Geithman (1974), p. 110, for Costa Rica.

Internal migration in developing countries

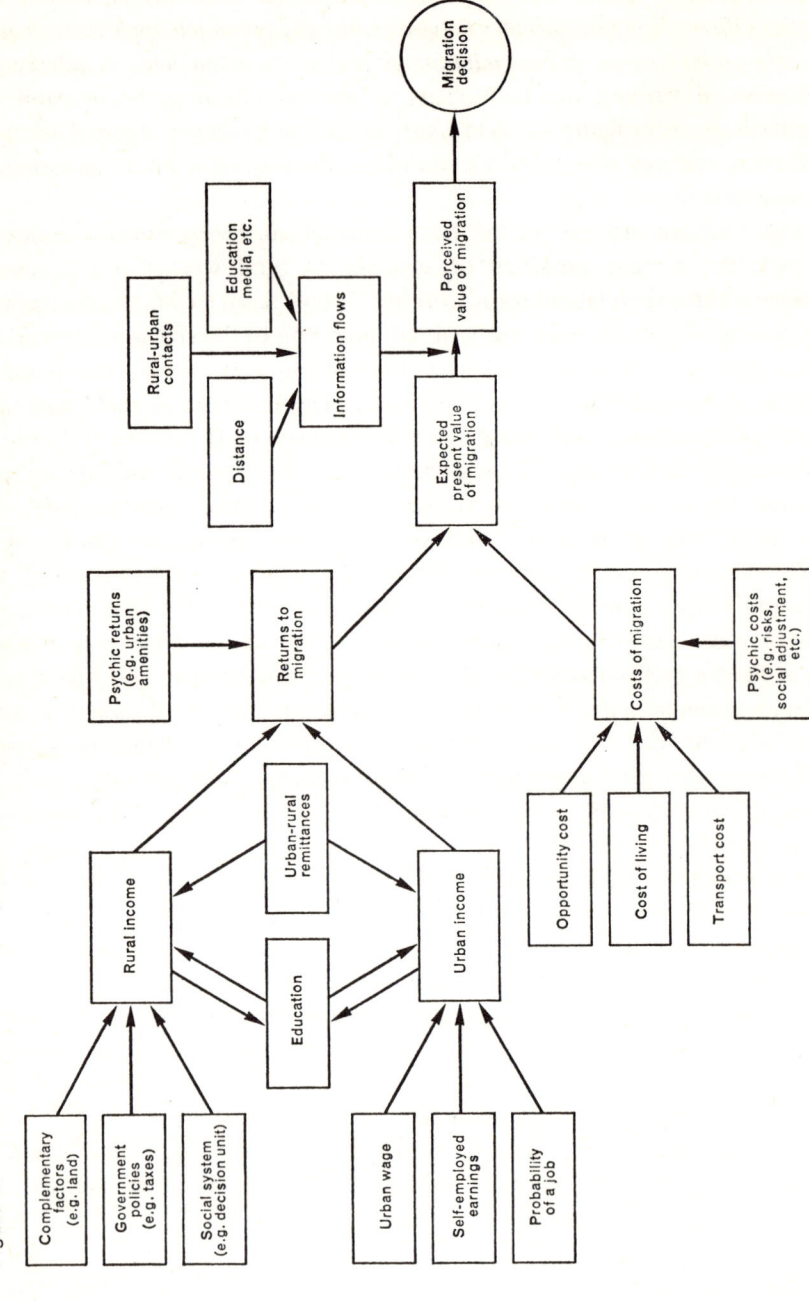

Figure 4. A framework for the analysis of the decision to migrate

Source: Byerlee (1974), p. 553.

real incomes. The fact that our hypothetical migrant can expect to earn twice the annual real income in an urban area as in his rural environment may be of little consequence if his actual *probability* of securing the higher paying job within the one-year period is one chance in five. In such a situation Todaro notes that the migrant's actual probability of being successful in securing the higher paying urban job is 20 per cent, so that his "expected" urban income for the one-year period is in fact 20 units and not the 100 units that a migrant in a full-employment urban environment might expect to receive. Thus, with a one-period time horizon and a probability of success of 20 per cent it would be irrational for this migrant to seek an urban job, even though the differential between urban and rural earnings capacity is 100 per cent. On the other hand, if the probability of success were, say, 60 per cent, so that the expected urban income were 60 units, then it would be entirely rational for such a migrant with his one-period time horizon to try his luck in the urban job "lottery" even though urban unemployment may be extremely high.[1]

Returning now to the more realistic situation of longer time horizons for potential migrants, especially in view of the fact that the vast majority are between the ages of 15 and 24, Todaro argues that the decision to migrate should be represented on the basis of a "permanent income" calculation. If the migrant anticipates a relatively low probability of finding regular wage employment in the initial period but expects this probability to increase over time as he is able to broaden his urban contacts, it would still be rational for him to migrate, even though expected urban income during the initial period or periods might be lower than expected rural income.[2] As long as the present value of the net stream of expected urban income over the migrant's planning horizon exceeds that of the expected rural income, the decision to migrate is economically justified. This, in essence, is the "thought process" that is schematically depicted in figure 4.

Rather than advocating wage adjustments bringing about an equilibrium between urban and rural incomes, as would be the case in a competitive model, Todaro argues that rural-urban migration itself must act as the ultimate equilibrating force. With urban wages assumed to be inflexible in a downward direction, rural and urban "expected" incomes can be equalised only by falling

---

[1] Clearly, the final decision will be influenced by migrant attitudes towards risk and uncertainty. Different migrants might react differently to the same expected urban income, depending on whether the probability of success is high or low — i.e. a 90 per cent chance of earning 100 urban income units might be perceived as more desirable than, say, a 50 per cent chance of earning 180 units. We shall explore this issue further in Chapter 5 when we analyse various econometric migration studies.

[2] The Hay (1974), Barnum and Sabot (1975) and Oberai (1975) studies, among others, provide evidence that migrant urban incomes tend to rise rapidly over time, especially during the first few years after moving.

urban job probabilities resulting from rising urban unemployment. For example, if average rural wages are 60 units and urban wages are institutionally set at a level of 120 units, then in a one-period model a 50 per cent urban unemployment rate would be necessary to vitiate the private profitability of further migration. Since expected incomes are defined in terms of both wages and employment probabilities, Todaro argues that it is not only possible but also probable for migration to continue in spite of the existence of sizeable rates of urban unemployment. In the above numerical example migration would continue even if the urban unemployment rate were 30 per cent or 40 per cent.

A mathematical formulation

Consider the following mathematical formulation. Individuals are assumed to base their decision to migrate on considerations of income maximisation and what they perceive to be their expected income streams in urban and rural areas. It is further assumed that the individual who chooses to migrate is attempting to achieve the prevailing average income for his level of education or skill attainment in the urban centre of his choice. Nevertheless, he is assumed to be aware of his limited chances of immediately securing wage employment and the likelihood that he will be unemployed or underemployed for a certain period of time. It follows that the migrant's expected income stream is determined both by the prevailing income in the modern sector and by the probability of being employed there rather than being underemployed in the traditional or "informal" sector or totally unemployed.

If we let $V(O)$ be the discounted present value of the expected "net" urban-rural income stream over the migrant's time horizon; Y_u, $_r(t)$ the average real incomes of individuals employed in the urban and the rural economy; n the number of time periods in the migrant's planning horizon; and i the discount rate reflecting the migrant's degree of time preference, the decision to migrate or not will depend on whether

$$V(O) = \int_{t=0}^{n} [p(t)Y_u(t) - Y_r(t)] e^{-it} dt - C(O)$$

is positive or negative, where

$C(O)$ represents the cost of migration, and
$p(t)$ is the probability that a migrant will have secured an urban job at the average income level in period t.[1]

---

[1] Clearly, the present value equation should be disaggregated further by age, education and sex as well as by regions of origin and destination, since both wage levels and job probabilities are likely to vary for migrants with differing demographic and educational characteristics (see below).

In any one time period, the probability of being employed in the modern sector, $p(t)$, will be directly related to the probability π of having been selected in that or any previous period from a given stock of unemployed or underemployed jobseekers. If we assume that for most migrants (i.e. with similar demographic and educational characteristics) the selection procedure is random, then the probability of having a job in the modern sector within x periods after migration, $p(x)$, is:

$p(1) = \pi(1)$

and

$p(2) = \pi(1) + [1 - \pi(1)] \pi(2)$

so that

$p(x) = p(x-1) + [1-p(x-1)] \pi(x)$

or

$p(x) = \pi(1) + \sum_{t=2}^{x} \pi(t) \prod_{s=1}^{t-1} [1-\pi(s)]$

where

$\prod_{i=1}^{n} a_i = a_1 \cdot a_2 \cdot a_3 \cdot \ldots a_{n-1} \cdot a_n$

and

$\pi(t)$ equals the ratio of new job openings relative to the number of accumulated job aspirants in period t.

It follows from this probability formulation that for any given level of $Y_u(t)$ and $Y_r(t)$, the longer the migrant has been in the city the higher his probability p of having a job and the higher, therefore, is his expected income in that period.

Formulating the probability variable in this way has two advantages: *(a)* it avoids the "all or nothing" problem of having to assume that the migrant either earns the average income or earns nothing in the periods immediately following migration: consequently, it reflects the fact that many underemployed migrants will be able to generate some income in the urban traditional sector while searching for a regular job [1]; and *(b)* it modifies somewhat the assumption of random selection since the probability of a migrant's having been selected varies directly with the time he has been in the

---

[1] A number of critics seem to have misread the original 1969 Todaro article by asserting that the author failed to take into account the existence of an urban "traditional" or "informal" sector by assuming that a migrant would be either employed in the modern sector or openly unemployed. But see Todaro (1969), p. 139, note 3 and Todaro (1972), pp. 49-51. Admittedly, however, there is some ambiguity and the implications of informal activities were not fully drawn out (see p. 41 below, modification by Fields, 1975).

Internal migration in developing countries

city. This permits adjustments for the fact that longer-term migrants usually have more contacts and better information systems so that their expected incomes should be higher than those of newly arrived migrants with similar demographic characteristics and skills (Todaro, 1969, p. 142, note 8).

Suppose we now incorporate this behaviouristic theory of migration into a simple aggregate dynamic equilibrium model of urban labour demand and supply in the following manner. The rural labour force L_R is assumed to grow at a natural rate r, less the rate of migration to urban areas m, or

(1) $$\dot{L}_R = (r-m) L_R$$

where $\dot{L}_R$ is the time derivative of L_R.

The urban labour force L_u also grows at a rate r, plus the migration from the rural areas

(2) $$\dot{L}_u = rL_u + mL_R$$

or substituting $M = mL_R$ where M represents the actual amount of rural-urban migration, equation (2) can be written as

(2') $$\dot{L}_u = rL_u + M.$$

The growth of urban employment opportunities (the demand for urban labour) is assumed to be constant at a rate g, so that

(3) $$\dot{E}_u = gE_u$$

where E_u is the level of urban modern sector employment.

So far the model is quite standard. The major innovation introduced by Todaro is his migration function which forms the core of the model. Todaro, as we have seen, assumes that the rate of rural-urban migration, $m \left(= \dfrac{M}{L_R} \right)$, is a function primarily of *(a)* the *probability* that an urban labourer can successfully find a modern sector job which in its most elementary form can be written as some simple (positive) monotonic function of the current urban employment rate $\left(\dfrac{E_u}{L_u} \right)$ or a negative function of the urban unemployment rate, $\dfrac{L_u - E_u}{L_u}$, and *(b)* the *urban-rural real income differential* which can be expressed as a ratio $\dfrac{Y_u}{Y_R} = W$, where $W > 1$ and is assumed to be fixed as a result of an institutionally determined urban wage and a given rural average product; migration will also be related to *(c) other* factors, Z, such as distance, personal contacts, urban amenities, etc., which also exert some influence on the migrant's perception of the relative "costs" and "benefits" of origin and destination opportunities. The basic Todaro migration equation can therefore be written as

(4) $$m = F\left(\frac{E_u}{L_u}, W, Z\right)$$

where $F'\left(\frac{E_u}{L_u}\right) > 0$; $F'(W) > 0$ and $F'(Z) \gtrless 0$.

Holding W and Z constant, the function F can be simplified to read

(5) $$F\left(\frac{E_u}{L_u}, W, Z\right) = f\left(\frac{E_u}{L_u}\right)$$

where $f' \geq 0$ for all values of $\frac{E_u}{L_u}$ between 0 and 1.

The substitution of equations (4) and (5) into equation (2) yields the basic differential equation for urban labour force growth in the Todaro model, namely

(6) $$\frac{\dot{L}_u}{L_u} = r + \frac{L_R}{L_u} f\left(\frac{E_u}{L_u}\right).$$

By then comparing the time path of this equation with the growth rate of urban employment, Todaro is able to discuss the dynamic process of rural-urban migration and urban unemployment under differing assumptions about population and employment growth rates (see Todaro, 1969 and 1971b (Appendix)).

However, the main attribute of this mathematical model is its rigorous demonstration that migration in excess of the growth of urban job opportunities not only is privately rational from the point of view of individual income maximising but also will continue to exist so long as the "expected" urban-rural real income differential remains positive. For any given relative real wage differential ($W > 1$), there will exist some urban unemployment rate that will finally equilibrate urban and rural "expected" incomes. But if the relative wage differential continues to grow (as it has in most developing nations) and if real urban wages are inflexible downward (as they have proved to be throughout the Third World), the rising rates of urban unemployment may never actually be able to exert their ultimate equilibrating influence on migration streams. On the contrary, continued and even accelerated rates of rural-urban migration can and will continue to exist simultaneously with these ever higher levels of urban unemployment.

In summary, there are four essential features of the basic Todaro migration model that should be kept in mind.

(1) Migration is stimulated primarily by rational economic considerations of relative benefits and costs, mostly financial but also psychological.
(2) The decision to migrate depends on "expected" rather than actual urban-rural real wage differentials where the "expected" differential is determined by the interaction of two variables, the actual urban-rural wage differential

and the probability of successfully obtaining employment in the urban modern sector.

(3) The probability of obtaining an urban job is inversely related to the urban unemployment rate.

(4) Migration rates in excess of urban job opportunity growth rates are not only possible but also rational and probable in the face of continued positive urban-rural *expected* income differentials. High rates of urban unemployment are therefore inevitable outcomes of the serious imbalances of economic opportunities between urban and rural areas of most underdeveloped countries.

Modifications of the basic Todaro model

There have been a number of important modifications of the basic Todaro migration model since it first appeared as a Ph.D. thesis in 1967. Many of these modifications were designed to introduce certain elements of reality into the migration process, elements which were assumed away or not taken into explicit account in the original Todaro model. But, by and large, the basic features of the model remain intact to this day and they provide the framework for most contemporary econometric migration studies (see Chapter 5 below). Among the major modifications of the original model, the following are perhaps among the most significant.

Harris-Todaro (1970)

First, Todaro and his colleague John Harris utilised and extended the basic Todaro framework to construct a two-sector internal trade model of migration and unemployment which made it possible to give explicit attention to the impact of migration on rural incomes, urban and rural output and total social welfare (Harris and Todaro, 1970). The two sectors are the permanent urban and the rural. The sectors are distinguished for analytical purposes from the viewpoint of production and incomes. Thus it is assumed that the rural sector specialises in the production of agricultural goods, part of which are traded to the urban sector in return for the manufactured goods in which it specialises. It is assumed further that the rural sector has the choice between using all available labour to produce agricultural goods (some of which are traded for urban manufactured goods) or using only part of its labour to produce food while "exporting" the remaining labour to the urban sector (i.e. through migration) in return for wages paid in the form of manufactured goods. Thus it is assumed that the typical migrant retains his or her ties with the rural sector. The income that he or she earns is assumed for analytical purposes to accrue to the rural sector. Such an assumption is clearly more valid for most African countries than for Asia or Latin America where migrant ties to the rural sector are less pronounced.

Although the above assumptions about intersectoral linkages enable Harris and Todaro to assess the welfare and distributional consequences of migration, they are not necessary for demonstrating the private rationality of continued migration in the face of rising urban unemployment. The crucial assumption for this proposition is once again Todaro's hypothesis that rural-urban migration will continue so long as the "expected" urban real income (i.e. the wage times the probability of finding a job) exceeds real agricultural income at the margin — i.e. potential rural migrants behave as maximisers of expected utility.

The complete Harris-Todaro model then represents a simple extension of traditional two-sector neoclassical trade models. Thus there are variable proportions of agricultural and manufacturing production technologies for the rural and urban sectors, neoclassical behavioural rules for the determination of levels of factor use and output in each sector, and a traditional trade theory mechanism for determining the terms of trade between agricultural and manufactured goods. But it is the migration equation which represents the unique and most innovative feature of the over-all model.

Harris and Todaro then utilise their internal trade-cum-migration model to deduce a number of policy implications for developing countries. First they evaluate the welfare effects (in terms of lost or gained output in each sector) of alternative urban employment policies, for instance uniform or sector-specific wage subsidies, urban demand expansion and migration restriction (see Bhagwati and Srinivasan, 1974, below for a critique of some of this analysis). Second, and more important, they draw attention to the critical importance of urban wage determination, commodity pricing policies and rural development programmes on relative output levels, the terms of trade and intersectoral labour allocation as a result of induced migration. Perhaps most important, the Harris-Todaro model shows that accelerated urban employment creation may actually increase levels of unemployment (see Todaro, 1976b, and below for a new theoretical specification and empirical formulation of this important concept of induced migration). Finally, they demonstrate the conditions under which coercive restraints on migration can actually reduce the level of rural welfare.

The mathematics of the Harris-Todaro model can be written as follows. Let W_R and W_u represent nominal agricultural and urban wage rates respectively, E_u the number of urban jobs and L_u the urban labour force. Expected urban income, $E(W_u)$, can then be written as

(7) $$E(W_u) = W_u \cdot \frac{E_u}{L_u}.$$

Expected rural income, $E(W_R)$, is simply W_R. The amount of rural-urban migration, $M = \dot{L}_u$, is, once again, a function of the urban-rural expected wage differential, i.e.

(8) $$M = \dot{L}_u = f(E(W_u) - E(W_R)).$$

The rural-urban equilibrium expected wage condition is then

(9) $$E(W_u) = E(W_R)$$

which becomes

(10) $$W_u \cdot \frac{E_u}{L_u} = W_R,$$

so that the Harris-Todaro model predicts as a first approximation an "equilibrium" urban *un*employment rate given by

(11) $$1 - \frac{E_u}{L_u} = 1 - \frac{W_R}{W_u}$$

or, alternatively, an employment rate $\frac{E_u}{L_u} = \frac{W_R}{W_u}$.

This prediction should not be taken literally as it is intended only to illustrate an inverse relationship between equilibrium unemployment rates and urban-rural expected wage differentials.[1]

While the combined Todaro/Harris-Todaro theoretical model does capture many of the most important labour market interactions between rural and urban sectors from the viewpoint of internal migration analysis, from the viewpoint of empirical or econometric estimation the basic model clearly requires some modification and extension. For example, Sabot has identified seven assumptions of the model which need to be modified to fit the institutional and empirical realities of certain developing nations. They are the following (Sabot, 1975d, pp. 5-6).

(1) Although the assumption that the urban incomes of migrants accrue to the rural sector is quite reasonable for many African societies with relative land abundance and strong extended family systems, it is less likely to apply to Asian societies where there are numbers of landless families and institutions of landlordship are prevalent.

(2) The assumption of homogeneous labour is not consistent with the universally observed selectivity by the migrant stream of particular subgroups of source area populations. The model must accommodate several types of labour.

---

[1] Such a literal interpretation of predicted "equilibrium" employment rates leads some critics (notably Fields, 1975) to overemphasise the apparent predictive inaccuracy (in terms of current available data on urban unemployment rates in developing countries) of the Harris-Todaro equilibrium condition and to overlook its important policy message regarding the inverse relationship between expected income differentials and urban unemployment rates.

(3) Similarly, the model assumes that capital stocks are given and that capital is immobile. This may be a reasonable assumption with regard to physical capital, but it is not so for forms of human capital investment (particularly education) that complement investment in migration. To assess the welfare consequences of migration the model must take into account transfers of human capital (see Corden and Findlay, 1975, below).

(4) The simple two-sector characterisation of the economy is inadequate since the choice of a migrant to urban areas is not merely between employment in the industrial sector and unemployment. There is a large "informal" sector that in fact absorbs a significant proportion of such migrants (Todaro, 1969). The relationships between such "flexible wage" sectors and the "rigid wage" modern urban sector need to be investigated much more closely than has been done to date (but see Fields, 1975, below).

(5) In addition, the modern urban sector is subdivided into two or more component labour markets with significant differences in the characteristics of employees and in incomes paid.

(6) Furthermore, the agricultural sector is hardly homogeneous, particularly in Asia where there is great stratification in land holding.

(7) Finally, the implicit assumption that information about alternative opportunities is everywhere available, accurate and costless to acquire is clearly inappropriate. The consequences of imperfect information systems must be taken into account. Associated with this is the corollary problem of financing a move. With the great imperfection of capital markets, many would-be migrants are unable to undertake moves that would otherwise be desirable. At least in Africa, the working of the extended family system is crucial to understanding how information is transmitted, risk of move is attenuated, and finance and supply for a move are provided.

Johnson (1971)

Johnson (1971) was one of the first to modify theoretically the basic Todaro/Harris-Todaro model by explicitly introducing variables for the rate of labour turnover and the possibility of the urban employed sharing their income with the unemployed through some form of extended family network. Thus Johnson defines the actual income in urban areas as $(1-\alpha)W_u + \alpha W_u n$ for the employed and $\alpha W_u n$ for the unemployed, where W_u is the urban wage rate, n is the urban employment rate and $\alpha (< 1)$ is the proportion of the total wage bill which is shared with the unemployed (Johnson, 1971, p. 22). Therefore, if p is the probability that an individual will be employed at a point in time, urban expected income at that time can be represented as

(12) $$E(Y_u) = (1-\alpha)W_u p + \alpha W_u n.$$

Johnson also introduces into Todaro's basic job probability formulation a variable to reflect the rate of labour turnover in the urban modern sector. Rather than new job creation being simply $g \times E_u$ (which assumes no labour turnover) the rate of new urban "hires" can be represented by

(13) $$\dot{E}_u = g \cdot E_u + \beta E_u$$

where β is the rate of job turnover.

Although β is probably much lower in developing than in developed countries, because of the scarcity of job opportunities in the urban sector and the fact that most people who leave a job do so only in the knowledge that another awaits them, Johnson's introduction of a labour turnover variable does bring the probability formula of the simple Todaro model a bit closer to reality.

Porter (1973)

Porter (1973) provides a further theoretical exploration of the dynamics of the basic Todaro model.[1] He attempts to demonstrate that urban unemployment cannot exist in equilibrium if employment in the urban sector is growing at a more rapid rate than the population as a whole while other factors are unchanging. In carrying out this demonstration, however, Porter observes that his theoretical modification of the Todaro conclusion "unfortunately for practical purposes ... offers no ground for optimism — the 'transitory' urban unemployment rates are depressingly high and long-lived" (some over 50 years). "Indeed, unemployment rates climb [to] more than twice as high as the 'equilibrium' rates estimated by Todaro ... for the same values of the parameters" (p. 1) and that "even a growth rate of urban employment several times the growth rate of population may be unable to reduce the urban unemployment rate to a tolerable level for an intolerably long time" (p. 15).

Bhagwati and Srinivasan (1974)

Bhagwati and Srinivasan (1974) provide an extensive yet on the whole positive critique of the Harris-Todaro model, identifying some of its theoretical weaknesses and modifying some of its major policy conclusions, especially those relating to the migration and employment impact of various wage and production subsidy programmes in both rural and urban areas. In particular, they point out that the Harris-Todaro conclusion that a (second-best) combination of an urban wage subsidy along with physical migration restriction would be necessary to achieve economy-wide production efficiency is not correct since a first-best solution can be realised by a variety of different tax or subsidy schemes, without the necessity of physical restrictions on internal migration.

---

[1] A somewhat similar but mathematically more sophisticated dynamic model of internal migration is analysed in Hoopengardner (1974).

Corden and Findlay (1975)

Corden and Findlay (1975) further extend the Harris-Todaro model by introducing intersectoral capital mobility between the rural and urban sectors in response to differentials in the return on capital. They also examine the comparative static effects of economic growth both in the original Harris-Todaro model and in the modified model with perfect capital mobility and with commodity prices determined externally in an open economy framework. They then explore the policy implications of the modified model and reach a number of conclusions which both support and modify those derived by Harris-Todaro.

Fields (1975)

One of the most extensive and useful modifications of the basic Harris-Todaro framework is that provided by Fields (1975). Fields uses the Harris-Todaro framework of quantity rather than wage adjustments as the principal equilibrating force in urban labour markets to consider four additional factors in the determination of equilibrium levels of urban unemployment in developing countries: *(a)* a more generalised description of the urban job-search process in which a rural resident may have some positive probability of finding an urban job without first migrating to the city; *(b)* the existence of underemployment in the urban traditional or "informal" sector in which workers are not barred from searching for a modern sector job although their probability of success is lower than for an unemployed worker who engages in full-time job search; *(c)* the likelihood that educated workers will be given preferential treatment in modern sector job hiring; and *(d)* the recognition of labour turnover in a multiperiod urban framework and the likelihood of differential attitudes towards risk aversion among different migrants. He shows that each of these realistic extensions imply a *lower* equilibrium urban unemployment rate than that "predicted" by the simple Harris-Todaro expected wage gap model (but see above, p. 38, footnote).

On the basis of his analysis, Fields suggests three additional policy variables beyond those suggested by Harris and Todaro and Bhagwati and Srinivasan which may have an important effect on the volume of unemployment and underemployment in developing countries (p. 185). These include: *(a)* the establishment of rural and/or urban labour exchanges designed to minimise the need for migrants to engage in costly (private and social) job search and thus to reduce the size of the urban informal sector, to lower open unemployment and to raise national output; *(b)* the (somewhat curious) recommendation that "over-education of the labour force might have the beneficial effect of both lessening urban unemployment and increasing national income in both the rural and the urban sectors" (p. 185) — this paradox arises because the more educated workers are selected first for jobs, thus reducing the probability that the less educated workers will successfully secure a modern sector job and thereby, through lower induced migration, reducing the number of potential migrants by more than the number of jobs taken by the better educated (via the Todaro induced migration multiplier); unfortunately, Fields does not take into account the "social costs" of over-education, especially in terms of forgone job opportunities, in his analysis; *(c)* the suggestion that it is *job hiring* rather than the *number* of jobs that primarily influences workers' locational decisions. Fields shows, therefore, that "a small increase in the number of jobs has a much larger proportional effect on job hiring and induces substantial rural-urban migration and increases the rate of unemployment. Thus migration can be stemmed simply by not growing so fast" (p. 186). This last policy conclusion echoes that made by Todaro in his original 1969 article but does not emphasise, as did Todaro's earlier article, the concomitant importance of generating a more rapid rate of *rural* employment and output growth.

Other (more recent) modifications

It is impossible to do justice to the burgeoning theoretical literature on internal migration in developing nations. However, among the more recent contributions the following deserve brief mention. Bookstaber (1976) extends the Bhagwati-Srinivasan paper further by exploring the policy intervention alternatives of the Harris-Todaro model when an average product wage is substituted for the more common marginal product wage in the agricultural sector. Among the more interesting conclusions is one stating that "two distortions are better than one — i.e. the optimal subsidy in the two-distortion case (average product rural wage distortion and urban minimum-wage distortion) is less than in the case in the minimum-wage distortion alone". This is because the required optimal tax to compensate for the average product rural wage distortion and the optimal subsidy required to offset the urban minimum-wage distortion tend to cancel each other out.

Steel and Takagi (1976), like Fields, examine some of the properties of the Harris-Todaro model when first an "urban intermediate sector" (productive small-scale enterprises using "non-modern" technology) is explicitly incorporated into the framework to give it three sectors, and then a rural non-agricultural sector and an urban "non-productive", "informal" sector (note the changing definition of the amorphous informal sector) is included to yield a five-sector model. Their main conclusion is that "the presence of an intermediate sector, which produces manufactured goods in small-scale establishments combining moderate amounts of capital with labour, substantially alters the two-sector analysis of the urban unemployment problem. When labour can choose only between agriculture, manufacturing and unemployment, any attempt to reduce urban unemployment by expanding job opportunities is likely only to aggravate it, through increased rural-urban migration. . . . This paper demonstrates that unemployment can nevertheless be reduced without sacrificing output growth (or at worst with very little cost), through expansion of the intermediate sector" (p. 21). However, in order to derive these results, Steel and Takagi are forced to assume that the marketable goods and services produced by the labour-intensive, small-scale intermediate sector "are perfectly substitutable for those of the large-scale, modern manufacturing sector" (p. 2). Unfortunately, it is difficult to think of many examples of "perfectly substitutable" goods and services between the intermediate and modern sectors, especially when account is taken of the "demonstration effect" of foreign products on local consumer preference patterns (e.g. for "wash-and-wear" clothing over simple cotton fabrics, for "perfumed" soap over the ordinary but less sweet-smelling variety, etc.).

Stiglitz (1976) expands on some of his earlier theoretical papers on migration (see Stiglitz, 1969 and 1974) to examine several characteristics of labour markets in developing countries which are important in determining the relationship between market wages and shadow prices for labour, particularly in the presence of a variety of rural and urban labour market distortions. On the basis of these distortions in labour allocation, Stiglitz generates a taxonomy of varying labour opportunity costs (defined as the forgone output of the government hiring an additional labourer in the urban sector) and the appropriate shadow prices necessary to maximise national output subject to a given capital constraint. He concludes that optimal wage subsidies depend on the form of the wage subsidies, that the optimal rate of wage subsidy is not equal to the difference between the shadow price of labour and the market wage and that shadow prices and market wages may be very sensitive to the hypothesis (e.g. rigid wages, efficiency wages, labour turnover, Cambridge hypothesis, etc.) made about the structure of the economy (p. 42).

Harris and Sabot (1976) attempt to assess the appropriateness of alternative macro-economic models (e.g. Keynesian and "structural") for the analysis of urban unemployment in developing countries. They conclude that the relevance of both Keynesian and structural models (in their optimistic and pessimistic variants) is constrained by their "inadequate attention to the micro-economics of labour supply" (p. 2). Harris and Sabot then proceed to argue that the "sectoral misallocation" model (i.e. the Harris-Todaro model and variants) is more appropriate for the analysis of urban surplus labour, especially in Africa. Finally, the authors argue that in situations where the sectoral misallocation model does not strictly hold, a more generalised "search" model similar to that developed by Fields (1975), and still based on the original Todaro assumption of a labour-supply function associated with "expected" economic returns, provides an adequate explanation of the phenomenon of urban unemployment in a wide range of developing countries, even where there is no aggregate imbalance between supply and demand in the urban labour market (p. 40). They therefore conclude that "the Harris-Todaro sectoral misallocation model is the special case of the general search model in which urban jobs are offered at only one wage ... and the potential migrant knows with certainty the probability that his search will be successful" (p. 44).

While probably closer to reality than the original Todaro or the subsequent Harris-Todaro models (which, at the time, had to make certain simplifying assumptions to get major new points across), the latest Harris-Sabot model suffers at the expense of the earlier models in that empirical testing is virtually impossible. For example, instead of an aggregate employment probability for each major age or educational group that can be estimated from census and especially survey data (see below) as in the Todaro/Harris-Todaro models, testing the Harris-Sabot model requires a knowledge of the "frequency distribution" of all subjective and objective employment probabilities as well as the range of alternative wage rates for each and every major category of rural migrant. As we shall see below, it is difficult enough to test adequately even the most simple version of the Todaro expected income migration model, given data limitations and survey research costs in most developing countries. Moreover, the policy implications of the Harris-Sabot framework are less easy to decipher than some of the other models reviewed in this section. Nevertheless, their model remains intellectually appealing and their work has certainly added to our understanding of the internal migration process and the dynamics of labour markets in developing countries.

Finally, in a recent paper Todaro (1976b) has attempted to develop a simple, empirically testable formula to explain the conditions under which an autonomous increase in urban job creation ostensibly designed to eradicate urban unemployment will, in fact, cause both the level and the rate of unemployment to rise. Using the basic Todaro model of rural-urban migration, the author derives the following policy-relevant formulae to serve as first approximations for the conditions under which

(1) the level of urban unemployment will rise:

$$(14) \qquad \eta_P > g \cdot \frac{E_u}{M}$$

where

η_P is the period-elasticity of induced migration with respect to changes in modern sector job probabilities,

g is the rate of urban employment growth prior to the autonomous rate of increase in new job opportunities,

E_u is the level of urban employment prior to the autonomous job increase, and

M is the existing level of rural-urban migration (also prior to the autonomous employment expansion);

(2) the rate of urban unemployment will rise:

$$(15) \qquad \eta_P > g \frac{L_u}{M}$$

where

L_u is the existing size of the urban labour force (again prior to the job expansion) and η_P, g and M are as in equation (14).

Todaro argues that if the observed, econometrically estimated period migration elasticities (η_P) exceed either or both of the above "threshold" values (i.e. $= g \cdot \frac{E_u}{M}$ for the level of unemployment and $g \cdot \frac{L_u}{M}$ for the unemployment rate), then governments intent on solving their urban unemployment problems through expanded urban job creation will actually worsen the situation if wage differentials remain unchanged. The simplicity of the above two formulae and the ready availability in developing countries of data on g, E_u, L_u, and M allows the author to determine *as a first approximation* what the elasticity of migration with respect to the probability of finding an urban job would have to be in order for this job-creation-leading-to-higher-unemployment paradox to hold in a sample of 14 developing countries. The finding is that they are so small (e.g. mostly ranging from -0.40 to -0.60) that the paradox can be expected to hold for most Third World countries. Todaro's calculations for these 14 countries are reproduced in Appendix 2, while the simple proofs of formulae (14) and (15) are derived in Appendix 3.

Conclusions

In spite of many significant modifications of the basic Todaro/Harris-Todaro model, the fact remains that its fundamental contribution — i.e. the idea that migration proceeds primarily in response to differences in "expected" urban and rural real incomes and that as a result of this the observed accelerated rates of internal migration in developing countries in the context of rising urban unemployment are not only a plausible phenomenon but are in fact entirely rational from the private "expected" income maximisation viewpoint of individual migrants — remains widely accepted to this day as the "received theory" in the literature on migration and economic development (Fields, 1975, p. 167; Jolly *et al.*, 1973, pp. 13-16; Meier, 1976, IV. C.1). This general acceptance at the "theoretical" level is reflected at the empirical level also by the widespread utilisation of econometric migration functions which give explicit recognition to the "expected" income differential as one of the most important explanatory variables in the migration decision-making process. In Chapter 5 we take a careful look at this growing body of quantitative migration literature in a wide range of developing nations. But first let us see how theoretical migration models have been translated into empirically testable econometric equations.

CONVERTING THEORETICAL MIGRATION MODELS INTO ECONOMETRIC EQUATIONS: A REVIEW OF ALTERNATIVE METHODOLOGICAL APPROACHES

4

In this chapter we attempt to summarise some of the major methodological issues relating to the conversion of theoretical migration models into empirically estimated econometric equations. We start off by distinguishing between "micro" and "macro" migration functions and their respective uses for information generation and policy analysis. We then provide a listing of those variables most commonly utilised in econometric studies on migration. Next we distinguish between the census and survey methodological approaches to estimating micro and macro migration functions, identifying the strengths and weaknesses of each but opting for the survey research approach as being more appropriate for future internal migration studies. We then discuss alternative field survey approaches including rural surveys, urban surveys and combined rural-urban field surveys with the objective of fitting means to ends. In this discussion we draw on examples of actual completed econometric studies based on these alternative survey approaches. We then examine the problem of estimating variables (both independent and dependent) in econometric migration studies focusing particularly on the estimation of rural and urban actual and "expected" incomes. We conclude this methodological chapter with a brief discussion of alternative econometric estimation techniques, including ordinary linear least-squares regression analysis, probit analysis, the polytomous logistic model, simultaneous equation (reduced form) estimation problems and procedures and some closing paragraphs on various uses of simulation techniques for migration analysis.

THE ECONOMETRIC MIGRATION FUNCTION: "MICRO" VERSUS "MACRO" ESTIMATION [1]

The fundamental assumption of all the theoretical and empirical literature on internal migration is the simple one that migration is the result *not* of

---

[1] For a more detailed analysis focusing specifically on estimation problems of migration decision functions, see Schultz (1976).

random selection or some arbitrary decisions of external authorities but rather of economically rational optimising behaviour on the part of individual or household decision-making units. Migration therefore is a *selective* procedure in which individuals with certain socio-economic characteristics and different sets of (mainly income-earning) opportunities are more likely to migrate than others. The major task of econometric migration research, therefore, is: *(a)* to identify the nature of these socioeconomic characteristics; *(b)* to devise appropriate measures of both characteristics and opportunities; *(c)* to specify appropriate relationships between personal characteristics, alternative economic opportunities and propensities to migrate on the basis of well formulated and plausible theoretical models; *(d)* to estimate the relative quantitative significance of different factors influencing either the propensity of individuals to migrate or the aggregate rate of migration; and, it may be hoped, *(e)* to be able to devise quantitative predictive estimates of the impact of alternative policy approaches designed to influence the magnitude of one or more of the independent variables identified as significant factors affecting the decision to migrate in a particular country or region.

Within this broad fivefold framework of objectives, econometric migration research tends to take on two principal but closely related forms: first, "micro", and second, "macro" functional estimation, as reflected in the choice of dependent and independent variables. We examine each in turn.

"Micro" function estimation

The "micro" economic approach to estimating migration functions asks the basic question "What is the probability or propensity that an individual will migrate from source area i to destination area j if he has certain demographic and socioeconomic characteristics and if differential economic opportunities in areas i and j can be specified?" Among the major demographic and socioeconomic characteristics of individuals usually considered in these studies are the following: age, sex, level of schooling, level of skills, range of personal contacts in destination region (through perhaps tribal, religious or ethnic affiliations of the individual). The economic opportunities in origin and destination areas are usually measured by farm income, non-farm cash wages, urban wage levels, job opportunities, etc.[1] In the absence of such direct information, levels of schooling, skills and personal contacts may be used as joint proxy variables for expected urban income by estimating "urban earnings functions" from available data (see, for example, Hay, 1974, and Mincer, 1974).

---

[1] See the section on "Problems of measuring variables in migration functions" below for alternative income measures.

Theoretical models and econometric equations

The dependent variable in the micro migration function, P_{ij}, is the propensity to migrate or, alternatively, the probability of migration from region i to region j. It is expressed simply as a binary, dichotomous variable taking on a value of 1 if the person migrated and 0 if he did not. Thus the aggregate estimated value of P_{ij} over all individuals will lie somewhere between 0 and 1 and the coefficients of the statistically significant independent variables will express the relative degree to which they individually affect a person's propensity to migrate.

Hay's study of migration in Tunisia provides a good example of the estimation of migration probability functions on the basis of, in this case, a rural sample survey of 220 households with at least one migrant and 80 households with no migrants (Hay, 1974). His actual sample consisted of 412 observations including 141 migrants and 271 non-migrants. The probability of migration that was estimated consisted of a binary dependent variable, either a migrant or not, as a function of a set of continuous and binary independent variables hypothesised to be determinants of migration. The actual estimated micro function and the hypothesised signs of the coefficients were (pp. 107-108):

$$P = f(S, \quad SK, \quad INF, \quad AGE, \quad AGE^2, \quad MAR, \quad HAMAN, \quad Y_c)$$
$$>0 \quad >0 \quad >0 \quad >0 \quad <0 \quad \gtreqless 0 \quad <0 \quad <0$$

where

- S = years of schooling and formal occupational training;
- SK = a dummy variable equal to 1 for those with job-learned transferable occupational skills and equal to 0 otherwise [1];
- INF = a dummy variable equal to 1 for those who knew someone who could help in obtaining an urban job and equal to 0 otherwise;
- AGE = age at the time of the survey for non-migrants and at the time of migration for migrants (age was hypothesised to be parabolically related to P — i.e. $AGE > 0$ and $AGE^2 < 0$);
- MAR = a dummy variable equal to 1 for those who were married and equal to 0 otherwise (at time of migration for the migrants); no hypothesis was made about the sign of this coefficient and, in any case, it turned out to be statistically insignificant;
- $HAMAN$ = the number of hectares per active man farmed by the individual household (a proxy measure of farm income);

---

[1] Hay used S and SK as proxy variables for urban expected income on the basis of an estimated urban earnings function for Tunisia. We will discuss this approach further in the section on "Problems of measuring variables in migration functions" below.

Y_c = annual rural cash income in dinars from wages and non-farm self-employment.

Hay used two methods of estimating the probability function: *(a)* a linear probability function estimated by ordinary least-squares (OLS) regression; and *(b)* probit analysis. Schultz (1975 and 1976) proposes the use of the polytomous logistic model as an alternative approach. We discuss various models and estimation procedures in the last section of this chapter.

"Macro" function estimation

A much more common and widely used procedure is to estimate the parameters of "macro" migration functions. The usual procedure is to estimate such aggregate migration functions where the dependent variable is typically the "gross" rate of rural-urban migration, m_{ij}, expressed as the proportion of population P_i that migrates to destination j over a specified period of time, so that $m_{ij} = \dfrac{M_{ij}}{P_i}$ where M_{ij} is gross migration.[1] m_{ij} may be further disaggregated by education, age, sex, etc.

Independent variables in macro functions usually include wage or income levels (Y) in i and j; employment (E) or unemployment rates (U) in j and sometimes i as well; the degree of urbanisation (Z) for the population in areas i and j; the distance between i and $j(d_{ij})$; friends and relatives of residents of source area i in the destination area $j(C_{ij})$; and perhaps also the size of the population (P) in areas i and j, although Z and P are likely to be correlated. The functional form of the migration equation is usually log linear (see Appendix A). Using the above symbols, its basic form and the hypothesised signs of the independent variables may be written as

$$\dfrac{M_{ij}}{P_i} = f(Y_i, \ Y_j; \ U_i, \ U_j; \ Z_i, \ Z_j; \ P_i, \ P_j; \ C_{ij}; \ d_{ij}).$$
$$<0 \ >0 \ >0 \ <0 \ <0 \ >0 \ <0 \ >0 \ <0 \ <0$$

Macro migration functions similar in form to that shown above have been estimated for most developing countries primarily from census data. In most cases the data has permitted the investigation of only interstatal or interregional migration rather than specifically rural-urban migration (see, for example, Beals, Levy and Moses, 1967; Levy and Wadycki, 1972a; Greenwood, 1971b; Sahota, 1968; Schultz, 1971 and 1975; Carvajal and Geithman, 1974; Wéry, Rodgers and Hopkins, 1974; and Falaris, 1976).

---

[1] Gross migration rates are usually obtained from present and prior residence data collected in a single cross-section, whereas net migration rates (the more desirable but very much more difficult variable for which to obtain accurate measures) can be estimated either by survival techniques linking two cross-sections with the aid of a life table or from survey data that "trace" return migrants in rural areas (see below).

A growing number of others, however, have utilised either survey or combined survey-census data (see, for example, Rempel, 1971a; Essang and Mabawonku, 1974; Hay, 1974; Huntington, 1974; Barnum and Sabot, 1975; Knowles and Anker, 1975; Oberai, 1975; Byerlee and Tommy, 1976; and House and Rempel, 1976). We discuss the pros and cons of census versus survey approaches below.

Both micro and macro migration functions represent important and necessary components of any comprehensive econometric analysis of migration in developing countries. Ideally, both types of estimation should be pursued.[1] However, in order to estimate specific micro probability functions, survey data are required. From a policy point of view each function can yield useful insights. The micro probability function can be used to estimate the impact of rising rural and/or urban incomes, increased educational levels and rising or falling unemployment rates on the propensity that an individual rural resident with certain characteristics will migrate. On the other hand, macro estimates of elasticities of migration with respect to changing urban and/or rural incomes, origin and destination, employment rates, etc., can serve as a basis for economy-wide policy formulation (see below).

Moreover, the macro function enables us to estimate the most important determinants of aggregate migration flows between two points i and j, to calculate the relative importance of these determinants and trade-offs between them (e.g. a higher destination employment rate against a higher destination wage premium) and to predict probable migration flows on the basis of estimated elasticity parameters. On balance, therefore, the macro approach probably has more *policy* pay-offs than the micro approach for the simple reason that policy-makers would probably rather have information on actual gross flows than on individual propensities. And yet, from the viewpoint of advancing our understanding of who moves and why, the micro propensity approach is more informative. Each approach therefore complements the other and they thus have separate and joint desirability in future migration research.

COMMON VARIABLES USED IN BOTH MICRO AND MACRO ECONOMETRIC MIGRATION STUDIES

Although there is great diversity among variables collected and/or estimated in different migration studies, by and large there does exist a certain core group of variables which are common to almost all the existing migration survey questionnaires. Such a listing of common variables is presented in table 6.

---

[1] In most cases, however, macro estimates of the parameters of gross migration functions are derived from aggregate data with the functional form itself being derived from a theoretical micro model of individual or household utility maximisation (see Schultz, 1976).

Table 6. List of variables commonly collected, with both rural and urban components, in most migration surveys

Sex
Age
Ethnicity
Status in household
Marital status
Number of children
Education

Variables collected by the urban components

Region of birth
Age on arrival in receiving area
Principal reason for moving
Year of arrival in town
Economic activity prior to migration
Income prior to migration
Intention to remain in receiving area
Expected reasons for leaving
Other migrants in family
Source of information regarding receiving area
Cost of transportation from source area
Source of finance for journey
Means of support on first arrival
Type of help from family and friends
Length of time to establish an independent source of income
Marital status on arrival
Location of wife and children at time of migration
Frequency of visits to source area
Current assets in source area
Value of remittances to source area
Current employment status
Type of employer
Occupation
Size of firm
Wage income received
Supplementary benefits
Year joined firm
Hours worked
Job-search procedure
Past employment experience
Self-employment income
Value of assets
Number of employees
Length of time in activity
Barriers to entry

Table 6 (continued)

Variables collected by the rural components
Income from self-employment
Non-monetary income
Value of equipment
Size of plot
Wage income
Employment history
Mobility history
Intention to move
Perceptions of opportunities elsewhere

Source: Sabot (1975d), p. 7.

Of the 50 or so variables listed in the table some are clearly more important than others for econometric estimation purposes (e.g. the income and employment status information). Others, however, such as marital status, ethnicity, sex, job-search procedure, intentions, expectations, and so on, provide valuable information of a more qualitative nature. All in all, the variables listed in table 6 provide a good summary picture of the range of information sought in most migration studies based on survey data and in many based on census information.

CENSUS VERSUS SURVEY APPROACHES: STRENGTHS AND WEAKNESSES

Although both the census and the survey approach to migration studies can offer valuable and useful insights into the migration process, most researchers would probably agree that the survey approach, supplemented where necessary by census information, offers the most promising avenue for future policy-oriented econometric migration research (see, for example, Schultz, 1976; Lipton, 1976; and Byerlee and Tommy, 1976). Among the many reasons for this viewpoint, the following are perhaps the most significant.

(1) Censuses generally collect information on "administrative" areas which in many cases include both urban and rural localities. They are thus more appropriate for inter-regional rather than for rural-urban migration.

(2) Field surveys, on the other hand, can be designed to classify information according to carefully delineated rural and urban areas. They thus facilitate the direct study of rural-urban, rural-rural, urban-rural and, where appropriate, even urban-urban (i.e. stepwise) migration.

(3) The degree of accuracy and coverage of census data may vary greatly from one census to the next. In particular, regional boundaries may be differ-

ently defined or sampling techniques may be altered. This is especially the case in most African countries (see, for example, Mabogunje, 1970). On the other hand, one of the main disadvantages of many field surveys is the occurrence of large sampling errors as a result of inadequate or inappropriate sampling techniques and/or a too small sample size.

(4) Most censuses often do not include information on income at the time of the census and their coverage of employment status is very weak. This greatly limits their applicability for testing alternative theories of migration, particularly in the case of those based on "expected" income maximisation. Their major usefulness is in recording migration flows by demographic and socioeconomic status.

(5) Field surveys, on the other hand, can be structured so as to elicit information appropriate to the testing of specific migration models.

(6) Census data quickly become outdated with changing socioeconomic conditions. Moreover, they provide only a cross-section at a particular point in time, whereas longitudinal information on various population cohorts is more desirable (Schultz, 1976, p. 5). Field sample surveys, however, can be conducted at more frequent intervals, thus providing both a more accurate time series and more up-to-date information, especially on the income-employment situation (Byerlee and Tommy, 1976).

(7) On the other hand, a faulty design of field surveys or the failure to carry out the design by inexperienced or uninterested interviewers can result in substantial sampling biases.

(8) When interpreting and evaluating the results of field surveys, however, several important considerations must also be kept in mind (Brigg, 1971, pp. 6-9):

   (a) is the universe being sampled a meaningful one — i.e. if just a portion of a country's rural or urban area is being sampled, is the sample representative of the whole region and/or other parts of the country? In many cases a poorly chosen sample will not yield meaningful information about the larger area of concern;

   (b) does the survey distinguish between independent and dependent migrants — i.e. between those who voluntarily move and those who accompany an independent migrant (his family)? Migration studies should in the first instance focus on independent migrants;

   (c) along the lines of *(b)* above, what is the appropriate decision-making unit in a particular area or region — the household, the individual or some combination of both? In many cases, failure to define the decision-making unit adequately and to interview the appropriate

(d) does the definition of migration distinguish between long-distance and local moves and how are these distances defined? Local moves may not necessarily reflect changing economic opportunities;

(e) how detailed and accurate was the questionnaire? Copies of questionnaires are rarely included in survey write-ups. Do questionnaires encourage incomplete answers or do they fail to cover an appropriate range of possible answers? Moreover, are the predesignated reasons offered to a respondent in answer to a certain question mutually exclusive and exhaustive, and is there space for volunteered answers? Although it is clearly beyond the scope of this book to enumerate the very many pitfalls of questionnaire design, pre-testing, testing, coding, tabulation, use, etc. (see, however, Byerlee and Tommy, 1976, table 1; Toosie and Scully, 1976; and Harris, 1976), the design of a meaningful and appropriate questionnaire is obviously a necessary condition for any migration study based heavily on field surveys to be of general use;

(f) since the field survey method is subject to problems of unreliable recall and emotional distortion by the respondents, it is essential that surveys distinguish between recent and earlier period migrants. Long-range retrospective information is notoriously unreliable, especially in the context of subjective questions about migrant perceptions and expectations at the time of the move. In general, qualitative measures (e.g. migrant satisfaction) should only be utilised in conjunction with appropriate quantitative measures and carefully constructed cross-check questions.

We may conclude that although census data can be "objectively" more accurate than survey data, their usefulness in contemporary econometric migration studies is greatly limited by (a) their failure to distinguish between rural and urban areas; (b) their usual failure to give adequate or any coverage to economic variables such as wages, self-employment, cash transfers, job probabilities, etc.; and (c) their tendency to become quickly outdated and to change their scope of coverage from one period to the next. Field surveys also have a number of inherent weaknesses but these can be overcome by an investigator's adequate knowledge of survey research methodology and techniques.

Future research on internal migration in developing countries, therefore, should be based very largely on the generation of primary data through the sample survey approach, preferably covering both rural and urban areas (see following section).

CHOOSING BETWEEN DIFFERENT SAMPLE SURVEY APPROACHES: FITTING OBJECTIVES WITH METHODOLOGY

The type of methodology employed and the choice of location for field sample surveys obviously depends on the model or set of specific hypotheses which the survey is designed to test. Data for econometric migration studies can be gathered exclusively in a rural sample area — as Hay (1974) did for Tunisia; exclusively in the urban area — as in Barnum and Sabot (1975) for Tanzania, Rempel (1971a) for Kenya or Harris (1976) for Indonesia; or in both areas with, say, initial interviews conducted in the rural area to identify migrants followed up by a "tracer" interview of these migrants in urban areas — as has been done by Essang and Mabawonku (1974) for western Nigeria, Nabila (1974) for Ghana, Knowles and Anker (1975) for Kenya and Byerlee and Tommy (1976) for Sierra Leone.

Clearly, the initial rural survey with urban tracer follow-ups is the most desirable methodology. A number of on-going migration studies are currently utilising this approach (see, especially, Byerlee and Tommy, 1976). Moreover, rather than relying on "one-shot" interviews, the ideal survey methodology would involve follow-up interviews at later periods in order to generate accurate time-series as well as cross-sectional information.

We therefore recommend the following three-step procedure as desirable in the organisation and conduct of future internal migration studies based on the field survey methodology.

(1) Initial survey information should be generated in representative *rural* areas in order to: *(a)* identify potential migrants still living in the rural areas and gain an idea of their perceptions about alternative economic opportunities; *(b)* identify actual migrants who have already left the rural household but who can be located in urban areas for follow-up "tracer" questionnaires; and *(c)* identify return migrants, to ascertain their reasons for returning and to try to calculate their economic "losses", if any, as a result of their migration experience. It is important that future migration studies identify not only actual migrants but also those who did not migrate, those who are on the margin' of migrating and those who did migrate but decided to return. At present there is no comprehensive migration study in any country or region that provides detailed information and analysis of these various components of the migration process. However, when it is completed the Sierra Leone study mentioned above will be among the first to provide such comprehensive information.

(2) As a major weakness of existing migration studies is the inadequate treatment and measurement of rural incomes (see the following section)[1], our

---

[1] The policy usefulness of many migration studies, for example Rempel's (1971a) study of Kenya, is largely negated by an inadequate treatment of rural incomes.

second recommendation is that, wherever possible, rural field surveys be supplemented by existing farm management or household budget surveys. In fact, the choice of an appropriate rural location to conduct the survey should, *ceteris paribus*, be dictated by the existence of such household budget or farm management studies. They can provide a valuable yet inexpensive source of additional information on average and/or marginal rural incomes by source and type of activity.

(3) Having interviewed non-migrants and potential migrants, our third step would be to "trace" as large a proportion as possible of those migrants who have been identified from the sample of rural households as having migrated some time in the recent past. Having located them in urban areas, information can be generated on their employment and income experiences as well as on other relevant factors (e.g. costs of moving and living, urban contacts, cash receipts and/or remittances to families in rural areas, etc.). These data can then be compared with similar information obtained about them through questions put to, say, the head of their households in rural areas.[1] This will not only provide a check on accuracy and consistency but will also give some idea of the relative marginal costs and benefits of urban tracer interviews for future migration studies.

PROBLEMS OF MEASURING VARIABLES IN MIGRATION FUNCTIONS

Measuring migration

One of the most difficult and persistent problems in utilising econometric techniques in migration research (or, for that matter, in almost any area of econometric research) is that of adequately measuring the major variables under review. In the case of the dependent migration variable, especially in macro functions, this problem is reflected in difficulties associated with the appropriate degree of aggregation, both geographical (interstate census data, for example, mask many different patterns) and demographic (which may hide the differential migration responses to the same stimuli of different subgroups within the population). Moreover, in point-to-point macro migration studies it is preferable to use a dependent variable which measures the proportion of people who moved from point i to point j during the year t rather than the people enumerated in point j in year t who were born in area i, as is done in most studies based on census data. The

---

[1] One of the methodological weaknesses of the Hay study in Tunisia, for example, was that all information on migrant incomes in urban areas had to be generated from interviews with the migrant's relatives in the rural area — i.e. there was no tracer follow-up in the cities.

latter measure is cumulative and may produce biased coefficients (Yap, 1975, p. 15) since past migration levels are likely to be influencing present wage and employment levels. Ideally, from an analytical and policy point of view, "net" annual migration flows would be preferred; but even where "gross" migration data are available for use as the dependent variable, there may still be some simultaneous equation biases since wages and (especially) employment levels both affect and may be affected by migration (see the following section). However, the sign and significance of the independent variables should not be too much affected by this bias, although coefficient sizes and standard errors may be influenced to a greater degree.

Measuring rural incomes [1]

It is with regard to the independent urban and rural income variables that many of the most serious measurement problems in econometric migration studies occur.[2] Accurate measurements are particularly difficult for rural incomes. Various studies have used different measures, including actual cash incomes, cash incomes plus some estimates of income in kind, net agricultural output per member of the rural labour force, or simply rural incomes per head. Knight has argued for Africa that the relevant measure of rural income varies according to the nature of the social system in the area. This typically includes the nature of the decision-making unit (individual or household) and the pattern of land tenure (Knight, 1972). Whether the opportunity cost to a migrant of leaving the farm can be measured by average or marginal value products depends on whether the household (average product) or individual (marginal product) is the decision-maker. Similarly, the land tenure system may dictate whether an individual is able to rent or sell his land or to retain a long-term claim to the land as a form of future financial security.

Normally one might hope to estimate rural incomes in "micro" migration functions by including a short farm management-type questionnaire as part of the interview schedule for households that own or operate farms. As an alternative, rural income may be divided into two components: *(a)* cash income from wages and non-farm self-employment; and *(b)* a proxy measure of the individual's share of income from the household farm. One such proxy measure could be the number of hectares of operated farm land per active man in the household (Hay, 1974, p. 94). This proxy assumes that farm income is equally shared and that a migrant forgoes his average product when

---

[1] For an extensive theoretical discussion of rural-urban income measurement problems in developing countries, see Collier (1976) and comments on Collier by Lal (1976); also Knight (1972).

[2] On the question of whether and under what conditions the absolute differences or the ratios of rural and urban earnings might best be used as independent variables, see Schultz (1976), pp. 14-16 and p. 25.

Theoretical models and econometric equations

he leaves. For any given individual, then, rural income will normally consist either of household farm and cash (farm or non-farm) earnings or of only one of these sources.

Measuring urban incomes: actual and expected

Urban incomes are normally easier to ascertain than rural incomes. If nothing else, one can obtain an estimate of actual wages from government statistics on average rates of renumeration in the modern sector by different skill categories. However, it is much more preferable if specific migrant urban earnings can be generated from primary survey data. In such cases, however, care must be taken to recognise the dual structure of most urban labour markets in developing countries — i.e. the coexistence of a modern, high wage (regulated) sector with a traditional (flexible wage) "informal" sector that is usually much larger. In most instances it will also be desirable to disaggregate urban incomes by educational and/or skill levels. Finally, it is important to obtain some estimates of private transfer payments (whether urban to rural or rural to urban) to arrive at more realistic estimates of "net" urban (and rural) incomes.

In the absence of reliable urban income data either from published sources or through a lack of sufficient responses to income questions in the survey, one could resort to the use of a "human capital earnings function" (Mincer, 1974) in which an individual's urban earnings can be estimated by a log linear regression of, say, years of schooling, level of training, experience, etc., on the current earnings of those in the sample who did provide income information (see Hay, 1974, pp. 89-104, for a description of this proxy method of estimating urban and rural incomes in Tunisia).

With regard to "expected" urban earnings, a job probability variable may be introduced separately or incorporated as a single measure of the urban expected wage (Barnum and Sabot, 1975, pp. 11-14). With regard to the probability variable, one would ideally like to have a measure of the ratio of the number of modern sector job openings (both new hires and turnovers) for a given job-search period to total urban surplus labour (i.e. the unemployed and underemployed — identified by an appropriate income measure — in the informal sector). Lacking this information, the probability variable may be measured for any job-search period (Barnum and Sabot, 1975, use four months for Tanzania) as the ratio of modern sector job openings to the number of unemployed or simply $p = \dfrac{g(1-u)}{u}$ where, as before, g is the rate of modern sector employment growth and u is the unemployment rate (which may be disaggregated by educational subgroups as in Barnum and Sabot, 1975, pp. 14-15).

A FINAL NOTE ON ECONOMETRIC ESTIMATION TECHNIQUES AND SIMULATION

Econometric estimation

As we saw earlier, almost all econometric migration studies, whether based on census or on survey data, use ordinary least-squares regression techniques, typically with logarithmic specifications, for estimating the parameters of both micro and macro migration functions. Some of the limitations of this approach, including sampling errors, problems of aggregation and measurement problems of both dependent and independent variables, have already been alluded to.

In the case of micro migration studies with dichotomous dependent variables there are a number of additional special problems associated with the estimation of linear probability functions using ordinary least-squares (OLS) regression techniques (Hay, 1974, Ch. VI). Normally the function expresses the probability of migration P, as a linear function of the independent variables

$$P_i = \beta_0 + \beta_1 X_{i1} + \cdots + \beta_k X_{ik} + \varepsilon_i$$

where

$P_i = 1$ if a migrant; 0 if not a migrant,

$X_1, \cdots X_k =$ the independent variables, and

$\varepsilon_i =$ a disturbance term.

$\bar{P}$ can be interpreted then as the conditional probability of migration for an individual with a given set of values for the variables $X_1, \ldots X_k$.

Among the objections raised against the use of OLS methods to estimate parameters of the above linear probability model are the following.

(1) It can yield predicted probabilities outside the acceptable 0–1 interval.

(2) The true probability relationship is more likely to be S-shaped rather than linear, approaching the limiting probability values of 0 and 1 asymptotically.

(3) The OLS assumption that ε_i is normally distributed and that $E(\varepsilon_i) = 0$ is violated when the dependent variable is a dummy — in the above case $P_i = 0$ or 1.

(4) In actuality, the var (ε_i) can be shown to be dependent on $X_{i1}, \ldots X_{ik}$ so that the OLS assumption of homoskedasticity is violated. Thus the OLS estimators of the βs are linear and unbiased, but not efficient.

(5) Finally, given the heteroskedastic nature of the error term, the OLS estimators, $\hat{\beta}$, will *not* be normally distributed and var $(\hat{\beta})$ is biased. Thus, t tests of significance cannot apply.

Given the serious limitations and statistical weaknesses of the linear probability function, probit analysis has been proposed as a preferential technique for estimating relationships with dichotomous dependent variables. Hay uses probit analysis in his estimation of the migration probability function for his Tunisian sample and demonstrates that this formulation more closely approximates the likely true function than does the linear probability function with OLS estimators (Hay, 1974, pp. 111-114).

Schultz (1975 and 1976) has suggested an alternative methodological approach designed to minimise several sources of bias that arise in studies of gross internal migration based on models of individual utility (expected income) maximisation. He proposes the use of the "polytomous logistic" or log linear model as applied in bioassay or more recently in economics (Domencich and McFadden, 1975) as a particularly desirable approach (Schultz, 1975, pp. 5-13). In the polytomous logistic model an individual is confronted with n alternative locations in which to reside (including his origin (birthplace) location, i). The probability that he resides in location j in a specific time period is assumed to depend on a vector of weighted personal and regional characteristics, Z_{ij}.

$$(16) \quad P_{ij} = \frac{e^{Z_{ij}}}{\sum_{j=1}^{n} e^{Z_{ij}}}, \quad \begin{array}{l} i = 1, \cdots n \\ j = 1, \cdots n \end{array}$$

where for each region of origin the probabilities sum to 1:

$$(17) \quad 1 = \sum_{j=1}^{n} P_{ij} \quad i = 1, \cdots n.$$

The set of Z_{ij}s is then specified as a *linear* function in natural logarithms of *(a)* the pertinent characteristics of the origin and destination regions (e.g. wages, employment rates, etc.) denoted as X_i and X_j; *(b)* the average distance between persons in the two regions, D_{ij}; and *(c)* "individual traits", Y_i, such as education, age, sex, etc., that affect the propensity to migrate. By stratifying the population according to these individual traits, the final functional form or "uniform" specification of migration as a single integrated decision process becomes as follows.

$$(18) \quad Z_{ij} = \alpha + \sum_{k=1}^{K} \beta_k \ln X_{ki} + \sum_{k=1}^{K} \gamma_k \ln X_{kj} + \delta \ln D_{ij}$$

$$i = 1, \ldots n$$
$$j = 1, \ldots n$$

where $\alpha, \delta, \beta_k, \gamma_k$ for $k = 1, \ldots K$ are the $2K + 2$ parameters of the migration probability function for each stratum of the population.

The uniform polytomous logistic model of migration summarised in equations (16), (17) and (18) can then be estimated by maximum likelihood techniques based on individual or grouped data. For those cells in which the expected migration probability is greater than 0 or less than 1, the model can be estimated by ordinary least-squares (Schultz, 1976, p. 35). Schultz utilises this estimation technique in his recent study of inter-regional migration in Venezuela based on the 1961 population census (Schultz, 1975).

While it is beyond the scope of this study to delve any deeper into the many problems associated with ordinary least-squares estimators of the linear probability migration function or the uniform logistic model, it should be pointed out that there often exist simultaneous equation biases in both micro and macro migration functions (Annable, 1972). This is especially true where wages, employment and migration affect each other in ways that make each variable endogenous within a larger system. In such cases simultaneous equation, reduced form and two-stage least-squares estimates are normally preferred to linear regression techniques.[1] Unfortunately, econometric migration research is still in its infancy so that we cannot as yet cite specific estimation improvements arising out of these more advanced techniques. We can only cite the theoretical weaknesses of OLS methods under certain conditions.[2]

Simulation

We may point out finally that the use of simulation techniques in migration analysis offers promising avenues for future research, especially when the general range of parameters for the most important independent variables begins to be better known. Two outstanding examples of the use of simulation for migration analysis can be found in Jones (1974) and especially Elek (1976). Porter (1973) also demonstrates the use of simulation in considering some of the dynamic properties of the basic Todaro model.

The use of simulation techniques by Elek (1976) to project future long-term rural-urban migration flows in Papua New Guinea on the basis of the Todaro expected income model is particularly interesting. Elek's over-all model is designed to simulate long-term changes in the population and economy of Papua New Guinea, particularly in response to alternative government strategies with regard to rural development, wages and incomes policies.

---

[1] See, for example, Stuart and Gregory (1974) for an analysis of Soviet migration using TSLS estimates. Falaris (1976) also uses simultaneous equation estimation techniques in his study of Peruvian migration.

[2] But see Hay (1974), Ch. 6, for a demonstration of the improved results arising from probit analysis and reduced form estimators over the linear probability migration function in the Tunisian case.

The population is stratified by age, sex, educational qualifications, location and workforce status or occupation. The over-all model is then constructed in modular fashion and consists of seven submodels (population growth, education, migration, allocation of workforce status, sectoral production and employment, personal incomes and expenditures, and government revenue and expenditure) linked to one another by a limited number of variables. This facilitates changes within any submodel (e.g. as a result of improved data or econometric investigation) without the need to alter the structure of the over-all model.

In particular, the migration submodel (Elek, 1976, Ch. 6) distinguishes three streams of migration (rural-urban, rural-rural and urban-rural) brought about by different influences (mostly rural-urban real wage differentials and changing job probabilities in different locations) and involving persons with different age, sex and educational characteristics. The parameters of the migration submodel were selected so that the projected streams of migrants were consistent with the observed net migration over the 1966-71 intercensal period in Papua New Guinea. The model focuses not only on new arrivals from rural villages but also on urban school leavers, others reaching working age, the urban self-employed (informal sector) and unsuccessful wage job-seekers in preceding periods.

Elek then calculates the discounted present values of "expected" net income streams for individuals with different demographic and socioeconomic characteristics in various localities under varying assumptions about government agricultural and urban wage policy, employer hiring practices (e.g. by education) and choice of techniques. Migration response functions by age, sex and education to "expected" income differentials were then used to generate a long-term geographical pattern of migration and a time path of urban unemployment levels and rates. Government policies that affect the rate of growth of wage employment or alter the differential between urban and rural expected incomes are shown to exert a direct and indirect influence on the process of labour force spatial adjustment. The long-term migration and employment effects of these alternative policies are explored by Elek in later chapters of his thesis. His simulations and sensitivity tests show quite clearly the importance of a successful rural development and urban wage strategy if substantial rural-urban migration and continuously rising levels of urban unemployment and underemployment are to be averted.

SUMMARY REVIEW OF QUANTITATIVE MIGRATION STUDIES   5

Having set forth in previous chapters a broad theoretical framework and a methodological analysis, we are now in a good position to review and summarise the results of completed migration studies. We first summarise the results of the "non-rigorous" descriptive migration literature and then look at the results of recently concluded econometric studies. Our main objective here is to determine what now seems to be known about migrant characteristics and the migration process in developing nations. This will allow us, in the next chapter, to delineate questions and issues that remain unanswered and therefore to suggest the most promising areas for future migration research.

SUMMARY RESULTS OF THE NON-RIGOROUS DESCRIPTIVE LITERATURE

Our best sources of information on the range of descriptive migration literature for developing countries are the earlier comprehensive surveys by Brigg (1971 and 1973), Carynnyk-Sinclair (1974) and, most recently, those of Connell et al. (1975) and Lipton (1976). Descriptive economic, sociological and demographic migration literature for a wide range of countries in Latin America, Asia and Africa was examined by Brigg, Carynnyk-Sinclair, Connell and Lipton. On the basis of these and other surveys (e.g. Byerlee, 1974) the following generalisations can be made.

Who migrates?

As pointed out earlier, migrants typically do not represent a random sample of the over-all population. On the contrary, they tend to be disproportionately young, better educated, less risk-averse and more achievement-oriented and to have better personal contacts in destination areas than does the general population in the region of out-migration.¹ In Africa the problem of migrant "school leavers" is widespread (Byerlee, 1974; Caldwell, 1969; Rempel, 1971a). While many migrants, especially in Asia (Lipton, 1976), are unskilled landless peasants, many others possess job transferable skills, have increasingly more years of schooling, and have some regular source of financial support for the period immediately following migration (Todaro, 1971a; Barnum and Sabot, 1975; Schultz, 1975). Although single men still appear to dominate the migration streams in Africa and Asia (Connell *et al.*, 1975), married men (many of whom are accompanied by the families) and single women are now more prevalent in Latin American migration patterns (Brigg, 1971; Herrick, 1971).

Why do people migrate?

The overwhelming conclusion of almost all migration studies, both descriptive and econometric, is that people migrate primarily for economic reasons. The greater the difference in economic opportunities between urban and rural regions, the greater the flow of migrants from rural to urban areas. While distance is usually a significant intervening obstacle, its negative impact can be largely offset by sizeable income differentials, especially for the more educated migrants (Barnum and Sabot, 1975; Schultz, 1975; Lipton, 1976).

In addition to the primary economic motive, people migrate *(a)* to improve their educational or skill level (also an ultimately economic motive); *(b)* to escape social and cultural imprisonment in homogenous rural areas; *(c)* to escape from rural violence and political instability; and *(d)* to join family and friends who had previously migrated to urban areas. Few studies seem to support the frequently heard hypothesis that migrants in developing countries are attracted to cities in search of better entertainment or "bright city lights".

What are the economic effects of migration on source and destination areas?

The quantitative evidence necessary to begin to answer this most crucial of all questions is almost non-existent in both the descriptive literature and in most econometric studies. It is thus a major priority area for future research (see Chapter 6). While there is no absence of hypotheses and/or conjectures about the relationship between migration and, say, rural development, such hypotheses are yet to be supported by anything more than casual empirical evidence (e.g. see Lipton, 1976). As pointed out earlier, internal migration was traditionally viewed as a socially beneficent process. Workers were shifted from low-productivity, labour-surplus source regions to high-

---

[1] For historical evidence on this point from developed countries, see Kuznets (1964).

productivity, labour-scarce destination areas. Seasonal migrants were able to supplement their incomes by short-term "circular" migration in accordance with seasonal variations in labour requirements (Elkan, 1960 and 1967). If real wages were imbalanced between two locations, the neoclassical price adjustment model dictated that in-migration would work to restore the balance by raising rural average incomes while lowering urban wages.

More recently, internal migration has been viewed less sanguinely, especially with regard to its effects on rural productivity *and* income distribution (Lipton, 1976). Rural-urban migration also appears to be accelerating in spite of rising levels of urban unemployment and growing numbers of "urban surplus" workers (Sabot, 1975b). Rather than adjusting downward to rising unemployment, however, urban wage levels continue to rise — mostly as a result of institutional rather than competitive economic forces (see, for example, House and Rempel (1976) for evidence from Kenya). While most studies show that individual migrants appear to be behaving in a privately rational manner, many observers now believe that internal migration adversely affects the welfare of source (primarily rural) areas (e.g. see Lipton, 1976; Connell *et al.*, 1975; Schultz, 1976; for a counter-argument, however, see Griffin, 1976). On the other hand, such migration seems to be contributing little, if anything, to expanded social welfare in destination (mostly urban) areas (Harris and Sabot, 1976; Todaro, 1976a). But, in spite of the growing acceptance of this "new view" of the contemporary relationship between internal migration and rural and urban development, little empirical evidence to support or refute this view convincingly can be gleaned from the descriptive migration studies reviewed in the Brigg, Carynnyk-Sinclair, Connell and Lipton surveys or in other descriptive studies. Clearly, more carefully designed studies of an econometric nature are required to test alternative hypotheses about the "net" social effects of internal migration on both source and destination areas.

To see if anything more can be learned, we turn finally to the limited but growing number of technically sophisticated econometric migration studies which have recently begun to emerge.

SURVEY OF RECENT ECONOMETRIC MIGRATION LITERATURE

Yap (1975) has provided one of the most extensive reviews of the limited but growing econometric literature on internal migration in developing countries. The econometric studies examined by Yap cover Ghana (Beals, Levy and Moses, 1967), Kenya (Huntington, 1974) and Tanzania (Barnum and Sabot, 1975) in Africa; Colombia (Schultz, 1971), Brazil (Sahota, 1968) and Venezuela (Levy and Wadycki, 1972a, 1973 and 1974a) in Latin

America; India (Greenwood, 1971a) in Asia; and Egypt (Greenwood, 1969) in the Middle East. More recently the following studies (not included in the Yap survey) have been completed: Kenya (Knowles and Anker, 1975; House and Rempel, 1976), Tunisia (Hay, 1974), Venezuela (Schultz, 1975), Costa Rica (Carvajal and Geithman, 1974) and Peru (Falaris, 1976).

All the above are cross-section studies, although Barnum and Sabot utilise both cross-section and time series data. Most explain point-to-point migration, usually between states or regions, although the Barnum and Sabot, Huntington, Knowles and Anker, and House and Rempel studies deal specifically with rural-urban migration. All except the Tunisia study considered aggregate flows between areas, and most utilised census data (again with the notable exceptions of Barnum and Sabot, Huntington, Knowles and Anker, and Hay). Most dealt with male migration only.

With the exception of Hay's micro probability function for Tunisia, explained earlier, all are "macro" migration functions. Typically they are specified in logarithmic form with the basic general formulation being

$$\frac{M_{ij}}{P_i} = f(Y_i, Y_j; U_i, U_j; Z_i, Z_j; d_{ij}; C_{ij})$$
$$i = 1, \ldots n$$
$$j = 1, \ldots n$$

where, as before

$\frac{M_{ij}}{P_i}$ = rate of migration from i to j expressed in terms of the population in i,

Y = wage or income levels,

U = unemployment rates,

Z = degree of urbanisation,

d_{ij} = distance between i and j, and

C_{ij} = friends and relatives of residents of i in destination j.

Capsule descriptions including regression results for the studies of Tanzania, Venezuela, India and Kenya are given in Appendix A.

The following is a summary of the major findings of these studies.

Importance of income and employment differentials

As might be expected, all the above econometric work demonstrates once again the overwhelming importance of economic variables in explaining migratory movements. Differences in average income or wage levels between two places invariably turn up among the most important explanatory factors. When income levels are included as separate variables, migration is positively associated with the urban wage and negatively related to the rural wage. When urban-rural differentials are combined into a single variable, the rate of migration increases with the size of the differential.

Importance of job probabilities and urban unemployment rates

Perhaps even more important from a theoretical as well as from a practical viewpoint is the finding in the Levy and Wadycki, Carvajal and Geithman and, especially, Barnum and Sabot, Knowles and Anker, House and Rempel, and Schultz (for more educated migrants) studies that the job probability variable appears to have "independent" statistical significance and to add to the over-all explanatory power of the regressions when isolated from the relative or absolute income differential variable (Levy and Wadycki, 1972a, p. 79; Carvajal and Geithman, 1974, p. 121, note 13; Barnum and Sabot, 1975a, pp. 17-18; Knowles and Anker, 1975, pp. 17-21; Schultz, 1975, tables 5c and 5d; House and Rempel, 1976). Thus, for example, Barnum and Sabot, in the first really comprehensive and significant test of the Todaro hypothesis based on a carefully designed sample survey, find that "the addition to the explained sum of squares in moving from the specification without probability to the specification including probability as a separate variable is significant at a 99 per cent confidence level" (Barnum and Sabot, 1975, p. 20).[1] Moreover, when the wage and probability variables are combined to form an "expected" wage variable, the result is a definite improvement over the nominal wage rate in terms of the amount of variation explained. Levy and Wadycki obtained similar results for Venezuela (1972a, p. 79) as did House and Rempel for Kenya.

These studies provide preliminary support for the Todaro hypothesis of the importance of the "expected" wage in migration, at least for Tanzania, Kenya and Venezuela — the only countries where, to the author's knowledge, econometric studies have given explicit attention to a separate probability variable.[2] It should also be pointed out, however, that Hay in his study of migration in Tunisia (1974) also confirmed the statistical significance of urban "expected" incomes; however, in the Tunisian case "urban earnings func-

---

[1] In his study of Kenya migration, Rempel (1971a) set out to test the Todaro model and found no independent significance for the expected "wage" differential or, for that matter, for the urban wage *per se* which in some regressions even had a negative sign! But, as pointed out earlier, Rempel's study surveyed only urban migrants, did not deal effectively with estimations of rural or, for that matter, urban incomes, had a statistically inadequate specification of the job probability variable and, in general, suffered from a number of other methodological weaknesses. To this extent, it was not a real test of the Todaro model. However, the more recent paper by House and Rempel (1976), as well as that by Knowles and Anker (1975) which was based on a more thorough sample survey of 1,074 Kenyan households in seven of Kenya's eight provinces, provide detailed support for the "expected" income hypothesis.

[2] Schultz's later (1975) study of Venezuela, using the same 1961 census data as Levy and Wadycki, finds the probability variable significant only for more educated migrants, while Falaris's study of Peru (which also includes an employment rate variable) reveals insignificant coefficients with the wrong sign. Falaris, however, points out that his results are flawed by problems over the measurement of census data as well as by simultaneity difficulties.

tions" in combination with proxy variables for urban expected income levels (schooling and level of skills) had to be utilised because data on actual urban income and employment rates were lacking.[1]

Urban employment expansion, wage differentials, job probabilities and induced migration

Job expansion and induced migration

An important hypothesis implicit in the original Todaro model and spelled out mathematically in the Harris-Todaro model concerns the "elasticity" of migration (i.e. the induced migration) response to changes in urban-rural wage differentials and urban employment probabilities. As indicated in Chapter 3, Todaro (1976b) has recently refined the concept and derived simple formulae (equations (14) and (15)) based on readily available migration, employment and labour force statistics for estimating the conditions under which an autonomous increase in urban job creation designed to lower both levels and rates of urban unemployment may in fact lead to increased levels and rates of urban unemployment. The outcome is shown to depend on two "threshold" values of the elasticities of migration with respect to urban job probabilities — a threshold level related to the amount of unemployment and one related to the rate of urban unemployment. Using secondary data for 14 Third World nations, Todaro estimates both threshold elasticities to be mostly in the range +0.20 to +0.60, although the unemployment *rate* threshold elasticity is always higher than the unemployment level elasticity (see Appendix C).

In this latest paper Todaro argues that if the actual econometrically estimated migration-job probability elasticity is higher than either or both of these threshold values, an expansion of urban employment opportunities can be expected, through the mechanism of higher job probabilities inducing additional migration, to lead to either a higher level, a higher rate, or both a higher level and a higher rate of urban unemployment. For example, in the Tanzania case, Barnum and Sabot (1975) estimate a migration elasticity with respect to job probabilities of +0.65 (regression No. 8, p. 21) which is well above the "threshold" level of +0.25 reported in Appendix B. Thus, as a first approximation, we may conclude that, *ceteris paribus*, an autonomous expansion of urban employment growth in Tanzania would be likely to lead not only to higher levels but also to higher rates of urban unemployment.

---

[1] In their study of Soviet rural-urban migration, Stuart and Gregory use the "tightness of the urban labour market" as a proxy variable for urban job probabilities and find it to be an "important explanatory variable" (Stuart and Gregory, 1974, p. 24).

Equations (14) and (15) and the illustrative computations reported in Appendix B therefore offer to policy-makers in developing countries a simple and convenient methodology using readily available data, for estimating, as a first approximation, the unemployment implications of policies designed to stimulate urban employment.

Wage differentials and induced migration

With regard to the impact of changing urban and rural wage levels on migration rates (i.e. the migration elasticity with regard to urban and rural wage levels), the studies by Huntington (1974), Knowles and Anker (1975) and House and Rempel (1976) for Kenya, by Greenwood (1971a) for India as well as those by Barnum and Sabot (1975) for Tanzania and Levy and Wadycki (1972a) and Schultz (1971) for Venezuela and Colombia respectively provide some initial evidence of the possible values of these differential elasticities. First, with regard to the relative importance of urban job probabilities compared with urban wage rates, the Tanzania study estimates that a given percentage increase in urban wages will induce twice as much rural-urban migration as the same percentage increase in employment (Barnum and Sabot, 1975, table 4, regression 7) while the earlier Venezuela study predicts roughly the same effect for interstate migration (Levy and Wadycki, 1972a, table 1). Schultz, however, finds employment rate elasticities of migration more significant than wage elasticities for migrants with some secondary and higher education (Schultz, 1971, tables 5c and 5d).

Table 7 provides illustrative data from the five studies cited above for destination and origin income elasticities of migration. In the two rural-urban studies (Huntington; Barnum and Sabot) the urban wage elasticities are higher than the rural elasticities, indicating that rural incomes will have to rise at a faster rate than urban incomes simply to offset the migration effects of a given increase in urban incomes.[1] Levy and Wadycki's interstate regressions for Venezuela show little difference between origin and destination income elasticities, while Greenwood's results for India show that origin wages are twice as important as destination wages — the reverse of the Barnum and Sabot study for Tanzania and the Schultz results for Venezuela.[2]

---

[1] Not much credence, however, should be placed on Huntington's urban and rural elasticity parameters since they are derived from Rempel's income data which, as we have seen above, are very deficient from a number of viewpoints. See, however, Knowles and Anker (1975) and House and Rempel (1976) for more credible results for Kenya.

[2] The Schultz and Levy and Wadycki studies illustrate one of the main problems of current econometric migration research: the limited comparability of results (even those using the same data base) because of different definitions and specifications of dependent (but also independent) variables. Clearly, the standardisation of these definitions and the adoption of more comparable measurement and estimation procedures is a prerequisite for meaningful cross-country as well as intra-country comparisons.

Table 7. Partial income elasticities, migration functions for men in selected developing countries

	Kenya (Huntington, 1974)	Tanzania (Barnum and Sabot, 1975)[1]	Venezuela (Levy and Wadycki, 1972a)	India (Greenwood, 1971a)[2]	Venezuela (Schultz, 1975)[3]
Dependent variable [4]	$\dfrac{M_{ij}}{P_i P_j}$	$\dfrac{M_{ij}}{P_i}$	$\dfrac{M_{ij}}{P_i}$	M_{ij}	$\dfrac{P_{ij}}{P_{ii}}$
Destination wage (W_j)	+6.79 [5] (4.61)	+1.26 [5]	+0.94 [5] (2.59)	+0.56 [5] (2.02)	1.83 [5] (4.33)
Origin wage (W_i)	−1.15 [5] (2.69)	−0.56	−0.85 [5] (2.32)	−1.24 [5] (4.48)	−0.857 [5] (1.96)

[1] Barnum and Sabot estimated a linear function, using lifetime earnings, undiscounted. The elasticities are calculated at the mean of the variables, using the income coefficients, 0.0024 (destination income), and −0.0070 (origin income).

[2] Greenwood's dependent variable is M_{ij}, rather than M_{ij}/P_i. However, the income coefficients would not change if his model were re-estimated, using the rate M_{ij}/P_j; for P_i, included on the right-hand side of the equation, has a coefficient of approximately 1. In other words, the income coefficient, α, is the same for

$$M_{ij} = Y^\alpha Z^\beta X^\gamma P^\delta$$
and
$$\frac{M_{ij}}{P_{ij}} = Y^\alpha Z^\beta X^\gamma.$$

[3] Schultz's dependent variable estimated by OLS in his polytomous logistic model is the natural logarithm of the *ratio* of the migration probability or the gross migration rate $\left(\dfrac{M_{ij}}{\sum_{j=1}M_{ij}}\right)$ to non-migrants, P_{ii}, used as the "numeraires".

[4] Definitions: M_{ij} = migration from place i to j
 P_i, P_j = population in place i, j, respectively.

[5] Significant at the 5 per cent level.

Sources: Schultz (1975), table 5a; Yap (1975), table 3.

Conclusions

Although the above information provides us with the beginnings of a policy-relevant econometric approach to migration analysis, it is only a beginning. A major priority for future research focused on rural-urban migration and based on carefully collected field survey information along the lines suggested in Chapter 4 is, therefore, a more scrupulous and detailed estimation of income and employment elasticities of migration for different countries at different points in time. From the policy point of view, a knowledge of such migration elasticities would go a very long way towards improving the empirical base from which effective wage, employment and income policies designed to induce a socially more efficient spatial allocation of human resources can be formulated.

Differential responsiveness of population subgroups and the effects of personal contacts and distance

The econometric literature in general supports most of the conclusions of the descriptive literature with regard to the differential responses of population subgroups to migration opportunities. More important, however, it provides quantitative estimates of the relative significance of these differential responses. The results can be summarised as follows.

(1) At the time of migration, most migrants tend to be both younger and better educated than those who do not move. Even when age is controlled for, migration and education are positively correlated.

(2) In Africa and south Asia men predominate (although female migration is increasing), while in the more urbanised countries of Latin America there is a growing excess of women over men in the migration stream.

(3) In each of the above cases (age, education, sex) economic motivations are paramount in the migration decision.

(4) The relative abundance of urban services and amenities do not seem to exert an independent positive effect on migration. The evidence on this point, however, is very tentative and fuzzy since none of the current econometric studies measures a migrant's utilisation of urban services. Furthermore, when including an urban amenity variable care must be exercised to avoid multicollinearity difficulties with other independent variables in the regression equation (e.g. wage levels, degree of urbanisation, population size, level of employment, etc.).

(5) Almost all studies show a positive correlation between migration rates (or propensities to migrate in the Tunisia study) and urban or state destination contacts in the form of friends and relatives. Such contacts can provide important information on job openings as well as lower the effective costs of the job search by offering costless or low-cost accommodation to the migrant (Fields, 1975). When contact variables are dropped from regression equations, however, the destination income elasticities remain significant and are reduced in size only slightly. Thus the presence of friends and relatives, while representing positive factors in a migrant's decision to move, are not substitutes for economic incentives.

(6) Finally, the negative effect of distance on migration, as predicted by traditional "gravity" models (Schultz, 1976), is pronounced in most studies. Migrants tend to move to cities and towns in their own state or region, but they will move over longer distances if the destination wages and job opportunities are considerably higher (House and Rempel, 1976). More educated migrants are therefore more likely to travel over longer distances than those with less education.

Private economic benefits of migration

With regard to the employment experience of migrants on arrival, their income gains and their economic status relative to those born in urban areas, the following information seems to summarise the evidence to date.

Private returns

Migrants on the whole do appear to have increased their private (and/or household) welfare as a result of migration in spite of high and rising levels of unemployment (Yap, 1975; Lipton, 1976; Carvajal and Geithman, 1974; Barnum and Sabot, 1976; etc.). By and large, many seem to have realised their private expected gains, although the proportion of "successful" migration appears to decline over time (Lipton, 1976). A number find regular employment soon after arrival and most seem definitely to improve their economic status over time. Quite a few start out in the informal sector before moving to formal sector employment (Hay, 1974). Many share part of their benefits with rural relatives through cash remittances (Connell *et al.*, 1975; Johnson and Whitelaw, 1972; Harris and Todaro, 1970; Adepoju, 1974; Sakdejayonto, 1973).[1] As Yap notes, however, "the proportion who have difficulty in finding work is probably greater than the reported number. They surveys use retrospective information, and the failures who left the area would not be included in the surveys" (Yap, 1975, p. 39).

Education and income

The studies reported here all strongly support the hypothesis that the incomes of migrants are highly correlated with education and skill level while being little associated with their status as migrants. To the extent, therefore, that migrants are more educated and have better skills than the average urban native, their incomes will be higher and their unemployment rates lower than urban non-migrants.

---

[1] A number of investigators, however, report substantial reverse (i.e. rural-urban) remittances (Connell *et al.*, 1975). In some cases it is argued that total rural out-remittances plus migrants' education costs greatly exceed in-remittances (Essang and Mabawonku, 1974).

LOOKING TOWARDS THE FUTURE: PRIORITIES FOR MIGRATION RESEARCH   6

Having carefully reviewed both the theoretical structure of existing migration models and the empirical information generated by the available descriptive and econometric literature, we are now in a better position to answer the question "What do we still need to know about the internal migration process and its impact on economic development?" The delineation of this "knowledge gap" enables us to formulate a list of research priorities which then provide the foundation for a comprehensive world-wide research programme focused on the causes and consequences of internal (and international) migration.[1] The following is such a suggested list.

MIGRATION AND DEVELOPMENT: A LIST OF RESEARCH PRIORITIES

Although our general knowledge base on the characteristics of migrants and the migration process, especially the paramount nature of economic factors in the migrant's decision-making process, is now well established, the literature on internal migration is only just beginning to explore, and even then rather unsystematically, some of the really interesting and crucial issues surrounding the migration problem. The major "knowledge gaps" which remain to be carefully and systematically researched, therefore, include the following seven elements.

(1) *Migrant perceptions, expectations and experiences.* How are migrant perceptions about job opportunities in potential destination areas formulated? Have their subjective perceptions been confirmed by experience

---

[1] Two major cross-country migration research projects are currently being carried out by *(a)* the Population and Labour Policies Branch of the International Labour Office, and *(b)* the Employment and Rural Development Division of the World Bank.

and, if not, how can the information system about destination job opportunities be improved?[1]

(2) *Characteristics of non-migrants, potential migrants and return migrants.* We know little about the job histories of return migrants and only slightly more about why certain people or groups of people do *not* migrate. Better information, generated by initial rural sample surveys followed up by urban "tracer" surveys, would widen the net of migration studies to identify not only actual migrants but also non-migrants, potential migrants and return migrants. Comparative information on all four categories could greatly broaden our knowledge base about migrant and non-migrant characteristics and the principal factors that influence their mobility decisions.

(3) *Importance of job probabilities and expected incomes.* In situations where there are positive income differentials between potential destination and source areas and an excess supply of labour in the destination area, does a separate probability variable related to destination unemployment (or, better, surplus labour) rates help to give a better explanation of differentials in migration rates? In such situations, what are the "private" (as compared with the "social") returns to migration? In short, do "expected" income differentials along the lines suggested in the Todaro models provide a better explanation of variations in migration rates and patterns than do simple "nominal" differentials? This crucial question needs to be researched carefully in future econometric studies.

(4) *Wage and job probability elasticities, induced migration and urban unemployment.* Perhaps the most important parameters in need of careful estimation in future econometric migration studies, at least from a policy perspective, are the partial wage and job probability elasticities of migration. By generating empirical evidence on the relative size of the destination (urban) and source (rural) wage elasticities as well as the (mainly) destination job probability elasticity both for individual countries and for a cross-section of countries, general conclusions can be reached about the relative importance of wage and job creation policies in affecting the size and redirecting the flow of migration into more socially desirable patterns. The linkage between migration policy and general development policy can be best revealed by knowledge of how diverse development policies directly or indirectly affect urban and rural real incomes and job opportunities and, therefore, influence the magnitude and spatial distri-

---

[1] Gugler (1974) argues for the use of employment exchanges and recruiting offices located in rural areas along the lines of the Mexican *bracero* programme to improve migrant information systems (see also Fields, 1975, p. 185 for a similar proposal).

bution of national and regional populations. Such a formulation of the migration question underlines the important two-way linkages between demographic and economic variables as expressed, for instance, in the ILO Bachue and other demographic-economic models (see, for example, Wéry, Rodgers and Hopkins, 1974).

(5) *The short- and long-term social and economic impact of migration on source and destination areas.* A major and persistent knowledge gap in internal migration studies in developing countries is the lack of detailed assessments of the social consequences of migration for both sending and receiving areas. In the case of internal rural-urban migration, the consequences of urban migration for rural source areas in terms of household income, productivity and opportunity costs for different rural subgroups (e.g. educated and uneducated, smallholders, landless labourers and peasant farmers as well as medium- to large-scale holders) needs to be carefully assessed.[1] On the other side of the coin, the consequences of internal migration for urban unemployment, the provision of housing, sanitation, health facilities and other social services, the social, political and psychic problems associated with urban congestion and slum developments and, finally, the relative impact of all of these on the welfare of migrants as well as of urban-born residents needs to be carefully and systematically examined. In both cases, better knowledge of the flow of private transfer payments in the form of the inflow and outflow of cash remittances will give us a better picture of both the short- and the long-run distributional impact of migration in terms of rural and urban household incomes.

(6) *The relationship between education and migration.* Although it is well known that more education increases the propensity of an individual to migrate, we are still unclear as to how much of this increased propensity can be explained solely by economic factors (i.e. more educated migrants have higher expected urban incomes because of both higher wages and greater employment probabilities, as demonstrated, for example, in Barnum and Sabot, 1975, table 1), and how much is the result of the impact of education on a rural individual's "world outlook". In other words, does education exert a non-economic, independent effect on propensities to migrate? It may do so, for example, by altering a rural individual's over-all utility function so that his "psychic" benefit/cost calculation of the private returns to migration works to reinforce his "economic"

---

[1] For suggested research priorities linking internal migration to rural productivity and inequality, see Lipton (1976) and Schuh (1976).

benefit/cost calculations. Those with more education, therefore, may have an "acquired" personality factor which causes them to respond disproportionately to non-economic as well as to economic incentives to migrate. Carefully designed survey questionnaires and well structured econometric models can help us to separate out these different effects of education.

(7) *Migration, income distribution and population growth*. The relationship between migration and income distribution, on the one hand, and migration and fertility, on the other, is probably among the least explored yet potentially one of the most significant areas of migration analysis within the broader context of economic and social development. Migration can have a direct effect on social welfare by altering the pattern of rural income distribution (Lipton, 1976) and thereby indirectly affecting the level of national fertility and future population growth (Kuznets, 1974). While the effect of migration on the spatial distribution of existing populations is a crucial issue, its impact on future population growth remains unexplored. There are a number of reasons, however, why we might expect migration to influence the geographical pattern and rate of population growth. First, migration affects the pattern of income distribution in rural and urban areas, and income distribution is thought to be an important determinant of aggregate population growth (Rich, 1973). In general, for any level of GNP per head, countries with a more egalitarian distribution of income tend to have lower fertility rates (Repetto, 1974), mainly as a result of the wider range of choice that more equitably distributed higher incomes bring to peasant families (Kuznets, 1974).

Unfortunately, in spite of some recent valuable descriptive studies (e.g. Connell *et al.*, 1975; Lipton, 1976), the relationship between migration and rural (as well as urban) income distribution is little understood. While migration may improve the private or even the household economic status of individual migrants (Griffin, 1976), it is not clear what its "net" effects are on aggregate rural incomes and production. Since migration is selective of the younger, more able-bodied, better-educated rural dweller, on balance the rural sector as a whole may stagnate as a result of the rapid depletion of its most dynamic human resources (Schuh, 1976). While individual families may be made better off, the sector as a whole may be made worse off. As a result, the existence of high rural fertility rates may be indirectly reinforced by the out-migration of their most talented elements. On the other hand, if economic incentives and higher income earning opportunities were promoted in rural areas, there might be the fourfold beneficial effect of lower rates of out-migration, less urban unemployment, higher rural incomes and potentially lower levels of rural fertility.[1]

All of the above is obviously very speculative, ad hoc theorising. But it does seem to suggest that a broader perspective on the relationship between migration, income distribution and population growth is in order. Future theoretical and empirical research on migration should begin to focus explicitly on this relationship as well as on the other six issues listed above.

---

[1] For a survey of the literature on labour policy and fertility in developing countries, see Ridker and Nordberg (1976).

SOME FINAL OBSERVATIONS 7

Bringing together all the preceding material on the nature and characteristics of theoretical migration models, the methodological issues surrounding the empirical estimation of micro and macro migration functions, the results of available published and unpublished migration studies (both descriptive and econometric) and the priority areas for future research, we may conclude by formulating a series of general propositions designed to strengthen the effectiveness of any proposed future research programme.[1]

(1) Emphasis should be placed simultaneously on the gradual refinement of the best and most widely accepted existing theoretical migration models, based both on the emerging empirical evidence and on the generation of additional empirical information by means of a few *parallel* carefully selected, judiciously conducted and well co-ordinated developing country studies.

(2) The empirical content of internal migration country studies should be based upon an agreed theoretical framework to be tested by means of the generation of primary data through the rural and urban field survey methodology outlined in Chapter 4. The same would hold true for the study of short distance international migration, e.g. from the Upper Volta to the Ivory Coast. If the study of long-distance migration is contemplated, field surveys are less feasible, and more reliance will have to be placed on census and other secondary data supplemented perhaps by mailed questionnaires.

(3) The policy content of statistical migration functions should be emphasised by more careful definitions of migration rates, wage and job probability variables, adjustments for possible simultaneous equations biases in

---

[1] Specific theoretical, methodological and research priority proposals have already been set forth in previous chapters and will therefore not be repeated here.

macro functions, and the use of probit as well as OLS regression analysis for micro propensity functions.[1] Larger disaggregated, cross-section samples of migrants, non-migrants and return migrants which are more representative of underlying rural populations combined with carefully collected time series information over, say, a five-year period would add substantially to the policy relevance of future econometric migration studies while not adding substantially to over-all research costs.[2]

(4) An attempt should be made to establish linkages between on-going migration studies to ascertain the possibilities for some methodological uniformity and to reap the economies of co-ordination in questionnaire design and other areas. As mentioned earlier, the World Bank has just initiated a project on rural-urban migration under the direction of R. H. Sabot (Sabot, 1975d). The World Bank project represents an attempt to organise into a research network a number of economic studies of migration currently under way in various African and Asian developing countries. The objective is to produce a monograph of comparative migration studies. While this project is much less ambitious, less systematically and methodologically organised and less clearly focused than that currently being initiated by the ILO, it would nevertheless be useful if there were some co-ordination between these two very different but very important projects. Although recommendations and even pleas for co-ordinated multi-disciplinary research on complex but highly inter-related development problems are ignored as often as they are put forward, in the case of current and planned research on internal migration a failure to link this research theoretically and quantitatively with development policy in general and population, employment and income distribution issues in particular would greatly limit the potential usefulness of its ultimate findings. We hope therefore that such a unique opportunity, which is of great importance to Third World population and development policy, will not be lost as a result of research scatteration when the social returns to research co-ordination appear so high.

---

[1] Schultz's (1975 and 1976) suggested use of the polytomous logistic model for estimating migration propensities also appears to be worth further exploration.

[2] For some representative cost estimates of this type of combined cross-section, longitudinal migration study, see Byerlee and Tommy (1976).

APPENDICES

A. SELECTED MIGRATION FUNCTIONS [1]

(1) H. N. Barnum and R. H. Sabot (1975): Rural-urban migration in Tanzania, 1955-71.

DEPENDENT VARIABLE : Male migrants by age and education categories in urban area j who came from origin region i as a proportion of the comparable population in origin i.

Migrant : Person in town j in 1971 who was born in the countryside and who moved to town after the age of 13 years.

FUNCTIONAL FORM : Linear.

DATA SOURCE : Migration from the 1971 national urban mobility, employment and income survey; population from population census.

Variables	Regression coefficients (t-statistics in parentheses)
Constant	0.11 (0.3)
Value of urban wage stream, undiscounted, by age-education group (using mean time of arrival for the age-education group)	0.0024 (4.0)
Value of rural per head income stream, undiscounted (monetary and subsistence income included)	−0.0070 (1.1)
Job openings in four-month job-search period as a proportion of number unemployed, by mean time of arrival	0.666 (4.1)
Average urban population in urban area j	0.023 (5.8)
Weighted average linear distance between receiving towns and sending regional centres	−0.0077 (2.1)
$\bar{R}^2$	0.55
Number of observations	108

Reference: table 4, regression 7, p. 21.

[1] Sources: Yap (1975), Appendices 1-4, for the Barnum and Sabot, Greenwood, Huntington and Levy and Wadycki studies reported here. Otherwise, data are taken directly from the studies themselves — i.e. for the Knowles and Anker study.

(2) M. Greenwood (1971a) : Interstate migration in India, 1961.
    DEPENDENT VARIABLE : Male migrants from state i to state j (M_{ij}).
                Migrant : Person who was born in state i and who has been living in state j for less than one year.
    FUNCTIONAL FORM : Log linear.
    DATA SOURCE : 1961 census of India.

Variables	Regression coefficients (t-statistics in parentheses)
Average annual income of workers in industrial establishments, 1961 :	
State i	−1.24 (4.48)
State j	0.56 (2.02)
Male population, 1961 :	
State i	1.01 (10.79)
State j	0.79 (8.46)
Percentage of male population residing in urban areas (5,000 or more), 1961 :	
State i	0.38 (2.52)
State j	0.16 (1.07)
Percentage of males who were literate, 1961 :	
State i	0.79 (2.93)
State j	1.11 (4.14)
Rail distance (kilometres) between representative cities and states i and j	−1.97 (16.18)
$\bar{R}^2$	0.70
F	59.8
Number of observations	240

Reference : table 2, p. 142.

Appendices

(3) H. Huntington (1974): Rural-urban migration in Kenya, 1964-68.

DEPENDENT VARIABLE: Male migrants who moved from province i to urban area j in 1964-68, as a proportion of the 1962 urban population multiplied by the rural population i ($M_{ij}/p_i p_j$).

Migrant: Person, age 15-50 years, enumerated in urban area j in 1968 who had moved during 1964-68 period.

FUNCTIONAL FORM: Log linear.

DATA SOURCE: Migration from a 1968 sample survey of 1,000 urban migrants, conducted by H. Rempel; population from the 1962 population census.

Variables	Regression coefficients (t-statistics in parentheses)
Constant	−44.23
	(6.00)
Average male modern sector earnings	6.79
	(4.61)
Rural cash income per adult male	−1.15
	(2.69)
Secondary school enrolment, 1966, as a proportion of population, 1969:	
Urban town j	0.901
	(1.35)
Rural province i	1.083
	(2.19)
Road mileage between urban town j and district centre i	−0.429
	(1.51)
Potential contacts (ethnic composition of urban area j weighted by ethnic composition in rural province i)	0.69
	(2.97)
R^2	0.61
F	11.2
Number of observations	39

Reference: table 5.1.

Internal migration in developing countries

(4) M. Levy and W. Wadycki (1972a): Interstate migration in Venezuela, 1961.

DEPENDENT VARIABLE : Male migrants from state i to state j as a proportion of the population in state i (M_{ij}/P_i).

Migrant : Person who has been living in state j for one year or less.

FUNCTIONAL FORM : Log linear.

DATA SOURCE : 1961 census of Venezuela.

Variables	Regression coefficients (t-statistics in parentheses)	
	Men 15-24 years	Men 25-54 years
Constant	−62.51 (8.61)	−19.52 (3.34)
Average wage of economically active males, age 10 years or over, 1961 :		
State i	−0.08 (0.19)	−0.85 (2.32)
State j	1.89 (4.69)	0.94 (2.59)
Percentage of economically active males, age 15-24 (25-54) years, who were unemployed, 1961 :		
State i	−0.21 (0.74)	0.73 (3.28)
State j	−2.45 (8.75)	−0.78 (3.47)
Total population, 1961 :		
State i	0.14 (1.18)	0.29 (2.69)
State j	0.98 (8.12)	0.73 (6.72)
Percentage of population residing in urban areas (2,500 or more), 1961 :		
State i	−0.72 (2.16)	−0.75 (2.49)
State j	1.10 (3.29)	0.81 (2.69)
Percentage of population, age 7-14 years, enrolled in school, 1961 :		
State i	3.07 (2.93)	1.14 (1.29)
State j	4.10 (3.91)	0.16 (0.18)
Road mileage (kilometres) between capital cities of states i and j	−1.06 (13.01)	−1.17 (15.92)
$\bar{R}^2$	0.61	0.60
Number of observations	380	380

Reference : table 1, p. 79.

Appendices

(5) J. C. Knowles and R. Anker (1975): Economic determinants of demographic behaviour in Kenya, 1974.

DEPENDENT VARIABLE: Whether person migrated (binary).

Migrant: Person, age 16 years or older, born in rural areas and now (1974) resident of urban areas.

FUNCTIONAL FORM: Linear.

DATA SOURCE: August 1974 survey of 1,074 households from seven of Kenya's eight provinces plus district and province level data.

Variables	Regression coefficients (t-statistics in parentheses)
Education	0.01167 (5.018) [1]
Age	0.00366 (1.506)
Square of age	0.0000 (0.077)
Sex (male)	0.00937 (0.574)
Land owned	−0.00291 (−5.154) [1]
Major roads (district of birth)	0.00111 (8.710) [1]
Expected earnings (earnings per head — district of birth) [2]	−0.01567 (−10.277) [1]
$\bar{R}^2$	0.075
F	28.44 [1]
Number of observations	2450

[1] Statistical significance at the 0.05 level. [2] The variable "earnings per head" is calculated as the product of two variables — earnings per employee (average earnings) and employment per head (employment rate). Earnings per employee is a measure of wage differentials, while employment per head is a measure of the likelihood of finding modern sector employment. Theory suggests that the appropriate district-level earnings variable would be the ratio of average earnings in a person's district of birth to average earnings in urban areas. Since, however, the urban average is assumed to be the same for all prospective migrants, the use of the ratio variable involves the division of average earnings in the district of birth by a constant, and is therefore superfluous (Knowles and Anker, p. 19, note 2).

Reference: table 6, p. 20.

B. SOME ILLUSTRATIVE ROUGH ESTIMATES OF "THRESHOLD" MIGRATION ELASTICITY COEFFICIENTS WITH RESPECT TO URBAN JOB CREATION, SELECTED DEVELOPING COUNTRIES, 1970 [1]

	g	$\dfrac{E_u}{M}$	$\hat{\eta}_P$ (Col. (1)×col. (2))	$\hat{\eta}_P^*$ $\left(\text{Col. (3)} \times \dfrac{L_u}{E_u}\right)$
	(1)	(2)	(3)	(4)
Africa				
Ghana	0.05	6.0	0.30	0.45
Kenya	0.04	8.7	0.348	0.47
Nigeria	0.035	9.0	0.315	0.47
Tanzania	0.03	7.0	0.21	0.25
Uganda	0.02	5.3	0.106	0.13
Zambia	0.04	10.0	0.40	0.58
Asia				
Republic of Korea	0.06	8.8	0.528	0.59
Malaysia (West)	0.07	9.2	0.644	0.82
Sri Lanka	0.05	9.7	0.485	0.71
Latin America				
Brazil	0.05	10.3	0.505	0.60
Chile	0.04	17.8	0.712	0.84
Colombia	0.04	11.5	0.460	0.59
Guatemala	0.02	8.0	0.160	0.23
Mexico	0.05	12.5	0.615	0.76
Peru	0.03	16.0	0.480	0.62

Source: Todaro (1976b), table 1.

[1] The reader is advised that the calculations in the table are extremely rough as they are based on published secondary aggregate data from a variety of sources (see below). They are intended primarily for illustrative purposes to show the probable range of η_P predicted by equations (14) and (15). A few such careful studies to check the predictive accuracy of these simple equations could have very high pay-offs in the long run.

Original sources

Col. (1): g is the rate of employment growth in the urban modern sector in both the public and the private sectors and is derived for different countries primarily from two main sources: Morawetz (1974) for the manufacturing sector alone, and United Nations (1974), tables 20 and 22 for non-agricultural employment and manufacturing. The figures are average annual rates over the period 1963-69 from Morawetz and 1968-70 from the United Nations source.

Col. (2): $\dfrac{E_u}{M}$ shows modern sector urban employment expressed as a ratio of the migration stream. Urban modern sector employment is estimated for each country by either calculating the size of the urban labour force simply as total labour force $(L) - L_R$ from ILO (1974), table A, or using actual urban labour force data from individual country sources. Where rates of unemployment and/or the size of the informal sector are known (e.g. for

Appendices

Ghana, Kenya, Nigeria; West Malaysia, Sri Lanka; and Colombia and Peru, from different sources), these are subtracted to estimate the size of employment in the urban "modern" sector including manufacturing, commerce, transport and general government. For other countries, E_u was estimated simply as 60 per cent of the urban labour force on the assumption that employment in the "informal" sector comprises approximately 25 to 30 per cent of the labour force while open unemployment ranges from 10 to 15 per cent. If anything, our estimates of E_u are biased upwards, with the result that our calculations of $\hat{\eta}_P$ are also slightly biased upwards. Migration data for each country are derived from Carynnyk-Sinclair (1974), tables 1, 2 and 3. Although the estimates in these tables are likely to be biased downwards, this is probably compensated for by the fact that the migration flows include a proportion of non-jobseekers (i.e. migrant families).

Col. (3): $\hat{\eta}_P$ is derived by using equation (10) simply as $g \times \dfrac{E_u}{M}$, or Col. (1) × Col. (2). Note that the estimated values of $\hat{\eta}_P$ in col. (3) are "threshold" levels of the elasticity. If the actual elasticity is higher than these values, the Todaro paradox of more urban employment leading to more urban unemployment holds. If actual elasticities are lower than these values but still positive, more urban employment creation will still induce additional migration so that the numbers of urban unemployed will decline, but by less than the number of new jobs created.

Col. (4): $\hat{\eta}_P^*$, the threshold migration elasticity for urban unemployment rates, is derived simply by multiplying col. (3) by $\dfrac{L_u}{E_u}$ for each country (i.e. the inverse of the modern sector employment rate), since from equations (10) and (14) we know that

$$\hat{\eta}_P^* = g \cdot \frac{E_u}{M} \text{ and } \hat{\eta}_P^* = g \cdot \frac{L_u}{M} \text{ so that } \hat{\eta}_P^* : \hat{\eta}_P^* :: E_u : L_u.$$

Data for E_u are obtained from col. (2) while data for L_u are derived from ILO (1974), table A, pp. 2-5, by using the agricultural labour force as a proxy for the rural labour force and subtracting this figure from the total labour force in 1970 for each country, so as to arrive at an estimate of the urban labour force.

C. A SIMPLE PROOF OF THE "THRESHOLD" URBAN JOB ELASTICITY FORMULAE OF EQUATIONS (14) AND (15) [1]

Let $U = L_u - E_u$ = urban unemployment *level*, and

$$\frac{U}{L_u} = \frac{L_u - E_u}{L_u} = \text{rate of unemployment.}$$

(1) Condition for the *level* of unemployment, U, to rise:

$$\frac{dU}{dL_u} > 0.$$

But

$$\frac{dU}{dL_u} = \frac{d(L_u - E_u)}{dL_u} = 1 - \frac{dE_u}{dL_u} > 0$$

or $\quad \dfrac{dE_u}{dL_u} < 1$

or $\quad \dfrac{dL_u}{dE_u} > 1$

or $\quad \dfrac{dM}{dgE_u} > 1\,;$

multiply by $\dfrac{gE_u}{M}$ and we have $\eta_P > g\dfrac{E_u}{M}$ which is the condition shown in equation (14).

(2) Condition for the *rate* of unemployment $\dfrac{U}{L_u}$ to rise:

$$\frac{d\left(\frac{U}{L_u}\right)}{dL_u} > 0$$

But

$$\frac{d\left(\frac{U}{L_u}\right)}{dL_u} = \frac{d\left(\frac{L_u - E_u}{L_u}\right)}{dL_u} = \frac{L_u\left(1 - \frac{dE_u}{dL_u}\right) - (L_u - E_u)}{L_u^2} > 0$$

or $\quad E_u - L_u \dfrac{dE_u}{dL_u} > 0$

or $\quad \dfrac{dE_u}{dL_u} < \dfrac{E_u}{L_u}, \quad$ or $\quad \left[\dfrac{dL_u}{L_u} - \dfrac{dE_u}{E_u}\right] > 0$

or $\quad \dfrac{dL_u}{dE_u} > \dfrac{L_u}{E_u}$

or $\quad \dfrac{dM}{dgE_u} > \dfrac{L_u}{E_u}\,;$

multiply by $\dfrac{gE_u}{M}$ and we have $\eta_P > g\dfrac{L_u}{M}$, which is the condition shown in equation (15).

---

[1] For a more precise description of these formulae see Todaro (1976b).

BIBLIOGRAPHY

Abt Associates Inc. 1970. *The causes of rural to urban migration among the poor.* Report submitted to Office of Economic Opportunity, Washington, DC.

Abu-Lughod, J. 1969. "Migrant adjustment to city life: the Egyptian case", in G. Bresse (ed.): *The city in newly developing countries: readings on urbanism and urbanization.* Englewood Cliffs, NJ, Prentice-Hall.

Adams, D. W. 1969. "Rural migration and agricultural development in Colombia", in *Economic Development and Cultural Change* (Chicago, University of Chicago Press), July 1969, pp. 527-539.

Addo, N. O. 1970. *Some structural aspects of internal migration in southeastern Ghana: their implications for national development policies.* Paper presented at the East African Conference on Social Science, Dar es Salaam. Mimeographed.

— ; Gaisie, S. K. ; Benneh, G. ; Kpedekpo, G. M. K. (eds.). 1969. *Symposium on Population and Socio-Economic Development in Ghana.* University of Ghana, Department of Sociology, Demographic Unit. Ghana population studies, No. 2.

Adepoju, A. 1974. "Rural-urban socio-economic links: the example of migrants in southwest Nigeria", in S. Amin (ed.): *Modern migrations in western Africa.* London, Oxford University Press.

Alers, J. O. ; Appelbaum, R. P. 1968. *La migración en el Perú: un inventario de proposiciones.* Lima, Centro de Estudios de Población y Desarrollo.

Andrews, F. M. ; Phillips, G. W. 1970. "The squatters of Lima: who they are and what they want", in *The Journal of Developing Areas* (Macomb, Ill., Western Illinois University), Jan. 1970, pp. 211-224.

Annable, J. E., Jr. 1972. "Internal migration and urban unemployment in low-income countries: a problem in simultaneous equations", in *Oxford Economic Papers* (London, Oxford University Press), Nov. 1972, pp. 399-412.

Balán, J. 1969. "Migrant-native socioeconomic differences in Latin American cities: a structural analysis", in *Latin American Research Review* (Austin, Tex., Latin American Studies Association), Spring 1969, pp. 3-29.

— ; Browning, H. ; Jelin, E. 1973. *Men in a developing society.* Austin, Tex., University of Texas Press.

Banton, M. P. 1957. *West African city: a study of tribal life in Freetown.* London, Oxford University Press.

Barnum, H. N.; Sabot, R. H. 1975. *Education, employment probabilities and rural-urban migration in Tanzania*. Paper presented at the 1975 World Congress of the Econometric Society, Toronto. Mimeographed.

—; —. 1976. *Migration, education and urban surplus labour*. Paris, OECD Development Centre.

Beals, R. E.; Levy, M. B.; Moses, L. N. 1967. "Rationality and migration in Ghana", in *The Review of Economics and Statistics* (Cambridge, Mass., Harvard University Press), Nov. 1967, pp. 480-486.

Berelson, B. 1974. *World population : status report 1974*. New York, Population Council.

Berry, R. A. 1975. "Open unemployment as a social problem in urban Colombia : myth and reality", in *Economic Development and Cultural Change*, Jan. 1975, pp. 276-291.

—; Soligo, R. 1968. "Rural-urban migration, agricultural output, and the supply price of labour in a labour-surplus economy", in *Oxford Economic Papers*, July 1968, pp. 230-249.

—; —. 1969. "Some welfare aspects of international migration," in *Journal of Political Economy* (Chicago, University of Chicago Press), Sep./Oct. 1969, pp. 778-794.

—; —. 1970. *National policy criteria in a world with international migration*. Houston, Tex., Rice University, Program of Development Studies. Paper no. 7.

Berry, S. S. 1970a. "The marketing of migrant labour services in African countries : a relatively unexplored topic", in *African Urban Notes* (East Lansing, Mich., Michigan State University), No. 3, pp. 144-153.

—. 1970b. "Economic development with surplus labour : further complications suggested by contemporary African experience", in *Oxford Economic Papers*, July 1970, pp. 275-287.

Bhagwati, J. N. 1974. *The international "brain drain" : an economic analysis*. Cambridge, Mass., Massachusetts Institute of Technology. Mimeographed.

—; Srinivasan, T. N. 1974. "On reanalyzing the Harris-Todaro model : policy rankings in the case of sector-specific sticky wages", in *The American Economic Review* (Menasha, Wis., American Economic Association), June 1974, pp. 502-508.

Böhning, W. R. 1975. "Some thoughts on emigration from the Mediterranean basin", in *International Labour Review* (Geneva, ILO), Mar. 1975, pp. 251-277.

Bookstaber, R. 1976. "Wage distortions and policy interventions in two-sector models", in *Sankhya* (forthcoming).

Bose, A. 1965. "Internal migration in India, Pakistan and Ceylon", in Office of the Registrar General, India : *Papers contributed by Indian authors to the World Population Conference, Belgrade, Yugoslavia, 30 Aug.-10 Sep. 1975*. New Delhi.

—. 1973. *Studies in India's urbanization, 1901-1971*. Bombay, Tata McGraw-Hill.

Bowles, S. 1970. "Migration as investment : empirical tests of the human investment approach to geographic mobility", in *The Review of Economics and Statistics*, Nov. 1970, pp. 356-362.

Bradfield, S. 1965. "Some occupational aspects of migration", in *Economic Development and Cultural Change*, Oct. 1965, pp. 61-70.

Bibliography

Brannon, R. H.; Anschel, K. R. 1970. *A re-evaluation of the contribution of the rural to urban labor flow.* Lexington, Ky., University of Kentucky, Department of Agricultural Economics. Mimeographed.

Brigg, P. 1971. *Migration to urban areas.* Washington, DC, World Bank. Staff working paper no. 107.

—. 1973. *Some economic interpretations of case studies of urban migration in developing countries.* Washington, DC, World Bank. Working paper no. 151.

Browning, H. 1971. "Migrant selectivity and the growth of large cities in developing societies", in National Academy of Sciences: *Rapid population growth, consequences and policy implications.* Baltimore, Johns Hopkins Press.

Byerlee, D. 1974. "Rural-urban migration in Africa: theory, policy and research implications", in *International Migration Review* (New York, Center for Migration Studies), Winter 1974, pp. 543-566.

—; Tommy, J. L. 1976. *An integrated methodology for migration research: the Sierra Leone rural-urban migration survey.* Paper presented at the World Bank Research Workshop on Rural-Urban Labor Market Interactions, Washington, DC.

Caldwell, J. C. 1968. "Determinants of rural-urban migration in Ghana", in *Population Studies* (London), Nov. 1968, pp. 361-377.

—. 1969. *African rural-urban migration: the movement to Ghana's towns.* Canberra, Australian National University Press.

Carvajal, M. J.; Geithman, D. T. 1974. "An economic analysis of migration in Costa Rica", in *Economic Development and Cultural Change*, Oct. 1974, pp. 105-122.

Carynnyk-Sinclair, N. 1974. *Rural to urban migration in developing countries, 1950-1970: a survey of the literature.* Geneva, ILO. World Employment Programme paper for restricted distribution only. Mimeographed.

Chenery, H.; Duloy, J.; Jolly, R. (eds.). 1973. *Redistribution with growth: an approach to policy.* Washington, DC, World Bank. Mimeographed.

Chiswick, C. 1974. *Identification of the urban poor: some preliminary results and hypotheses.* Washington, DC, World Bank. Urban Poverty Task Force paper.

Collier, P. 1976. *On the measurement of rural-urban income differentials.* Paper presented at the World Bank Research Workshop on Rural-Urban Labor Market Interactions, Washington, DC.

Collier, V.; Rempel, H. 1973. *The divergence between private and social costs in rural-urban migration: a case study of Nairobi.* Paper presented at the Canadian Economics Association meeting. Mimeographed.

Collins, G. R. 1952. "Movements of population from rural to urban areas in Sierra Leone with special reference to economic aspects and to the Colony rural areas", in *Record* (Brussels, International Institute of Differing Civilizations), No. 27, pp. 152-171.

Connell, J.; Dasgupta, B.; Laishley, R.; Lipton, M. 1975. *Migration from rural areas: the evidence from village studies.* Brighton, University of Sussex, Institute of Development Studies. Discussion paper no. 39.

Corden, W. M.; Findlay, R. 1975. "Urban unemployment, intersectoral capital mobility and development policy", in *Economica* (London School of Economics and Political Science), Feb. 1975, pp. 59-78.

Cuca, R. 1974. *Population growth, migration and concentration in Mexico* (draft). Washington, DC, World Bank.

Da Mata, M.; de Carvalho, E.; de Castro e Silva, M. T. 1973. *Migraçoes internas do Brasil*. Rio de Janeiro, Instituto de Planejamento Econômico e Social. Relatório de pesquisa no. 19.

Diehl, W. D. 1966. "Farm-nonfarm migration in the southeast: a costs-returns analysis", in *Journal of Farm Economics* (Lexington, Ky.), No. 1, pp. 1-11.

Diejomaoh, V. P.; Orimalade, W. A. T. 1971. "Unemployment in Nigeria: an economic analysis of scope trends and policy issues", in *The Nigerian Journal of Economic and Social Studies* (Ibadan, Nigerian Economic Society), No. 2, pp. 127-160.

Domencich, T.; McFadden, D. 1975. *Urban travel demand: a behavioral analysis*. Amsterdam, North-Holland Publishing Co.

Dorjahn, V. R. 1971. "The effects of labor migration on rural Liberia", in *Rural Africana* (East Lansing, Mich.), Summer 1971, pp. 51-65.

Ducoff, L. 1963. *The migrant population of a metropolitan area in a developing country: a preliminary report on a case study of San Salvador*. London, UNESCO.

Eames, E. 1965. "Urbanization and rural-urban migration in India", in *Population Review* (Madras, Indian Institute for Population Studies), Jan. 1965, pp. 38-47.

Edwards, E. O. (ed.). 1974. *Employment in developing nations*. New York, Columbia University Press.

—; Todaro, M. P. 1973. "Educational demand and supply in the context of growing unemployment in less developed countries", in *World Development* (Oxford), Mar./Apr. 1973, pp. 107-117.

Eicher, C.; Zalla, T.; Kocher, J.; Winch, F. 1970. *Employment generation in African agriculture*. East Lansing, Mich., Michigan State University, Institute of International Agriculture.

Elek, A. T. 1976. *A simulation model for long-term policy formation in Papua New Guinea*. Canberra, Australian National University. Unpublished Ph.D. thesis.

Elizaga, J. 1965. "A study of migration to Greater Santiago (Chile)", in *Demography* (Chicago, Population Association of America), No. 2, pp. 352-377.

Elkan, W. 1960. *Migrants and proletarians: urban labour in the economic development of Uganda*. London and New York, Oxford University Press.

—. 1967. "Circular migration and the growth of towns in east Africa", in *International Labour Review*, Dec. 1967, pp. 581-589.

—. 1970. "Urban unemployment in East Africa", in *International Affairs* (London), July 1970, pp. 517-528.

Engmann, E. V. T. 1965. "Population movements in Ghana", in *Bulletin of the Ghana Geography Association*, No. 1, pp. 41-65.

Enke, S. 1969. "Economists and development: rediscovering old truths", in *The Journal of Economic Literature* (Menasha, Wis., American Economic Association), Dec. 1969, pp. 1125-1139.

Essang, S. M.; Mabawonku, A. F. 1974. *Determinants and impact of rural-urban migration: a case study of selected communities in western Nigeria*. East Lansing, Mich., Michigan State University, Department of Agricultural Economics. African rural employment paper no. 10.

Falaris, E. M. 1976. *The determinants of internal migration in Peru: an economic analysis*. Minneapolis, Minn., University of Minnesota, Department of Economics. Mimeographed.

Bibliography

Farooq, G. 1966. *The people of Karachi: economic characteristics.* Karachi, Pakistan Institute of Development Economics.

Fei, J. C. H.; Ranis, G. 1961. "A theory of economic development", in *The American Economic Review*, Sep. 1961, pp. 533-565.

Fetter, B. 1968. "Elisabethville — immigrants to Elisabethville: their origin and aims", in *African Urban Notes*, No. 2, pp. 17-38.

Fields, G. 1974. *Migration, labor turnover, and human investment theory.* New Haven, Conn., Yale University, Economic Growth Center. Discussion paper no. 209.

—. 1975. "Rural-urban migration, urban unemployment and underemployment, and job-search activity in LDCs", in *Journal of Development Economics* (Amsterdam, North-Holland Publishing Co.), June 1975, pp. 165-187.

Flinn, W. L. 1966. *Rural to urban migration: a Colombian case.* Madison, Wis., University of Wisconsin, Land Tenure Center. Research paper no. 19.

—. 1968. "The process of migration to a shantytown in Bogotá", in *Inter-American Economic Affairs* (Washington, DC), Autumn 1968, pp. 77-88.

—; Cartano, D. G. 1970. "A comparison of the migration process to an urban *barrio* and to a rural community: two case studies", in *Inter-American Economic Affairs*, Autumn 1970, pp. 37-48.

Frank, C. R., Jr. 1971. "The problem of urban unemployment in Africa", in R. G. Ridker and H. Lubell (eds.): *Employment and unemployment problems of the Near East and South Asia.* Delhi, Vikas Publications.

—. 1971. "Causes and effects of migration in Africa", in *Association for Comparative Economics: Proceedings*, pp. 1-22.

Friedlander, S. L. 1965. *Labour migration and economic growth: a case study of Puerto Rico.* Cambridge, Mass., Massachusetts Institute of Technology Press.

Galenson, W.; Leibenstein, H. 1955. "Investment criteria, productivity and economic development", in *Quarterly Journal of Economics* (Cambridge, Mass., Harvard University Press), Aug. 1955, pp. 343-370.

Geiser, P. 1967. "Some differential factors affecting population movement: the Nubian case", in *Human Organization* (Lexington, Ky.), Fall 1967, pp. 164-177.

Germani, G. 1961. "Inquiry into the social effects of urbanization in a working-class sector of Greater Buenos Aires", in P. Hauser (ed.): *Urbanization in Latin America.* Paris, UNESCO.

Gessain, M. 1967. *Les migrations des Coniagui et Bassari.* Paris, Centre National de la Recherche Scientifique, Société des Africanistes.

Godfrey, E. M. 1973. "Economic variables and rural-urban migration: some thoughts on the Todaro hypothesis", in *Journal of Development Studies* (London, Frank Cass), No. 10, pp. 66-78.

Graham, D. H. 1970. "Divergent and convergent regional economic growth and internal migration in Brazil — 1940-1960", in *Economic Development and Cultural Change*, Apr. 1970, pp. 362-382.

Greenwood, M. 1969. "The determinants of labor migration in Egypt", in *Journal of Regional Science* (Philadelphia, Regional Science Research Institute), Aug. 1969, pp. 283-290.

—. 1971a. "An analysis of the determinants of internal labor mobility in India", in *Annals of Regional Science* (Bellingham, Wash., Western Washington State College), No. 1, pp. 137-151.

—. 1971b. "A regression analysis of migration to urban areas of a less-developed country: the case of India", in *Journal of Regional Science*, Aug. 1971, pp. 253-262.

—. 1972. "Lagged response in the decision to migrate: a reply", in *Journal of Regional Science*, Aug. 1972, pp. 311-324.

—. 1973. "The influence of family and friends on geographic labor mobility in a less developed country: the case of India", in *Review of Regional Studies* (Blacksburg, Va., Virginia Polytechnical Institute), No. 3, pp. 27-36.

—. 1975. "Research on internal migration in the United States: a survey", in *The Journal of Economic Literature*, June 1975, pp. 397-433.

Griffin, K. 1976. *The impact of migration from rural areas: comments on Michael Lipton's paper*. Paper presented at the World Bank Research Workshop on Rural-Urban Labor Market Interactions, Washington, DC.

Grimshaw, A. D. 1958. "Relationships between agricultural and economic indices and rural migration", in *Rural Sociology* (Pennsylvania State University), Vol. 23, pp. 397-400.

Gugler, J. 1968. "The impact of labour migration on society and economy in sub-Saharan Africa: empirical findings and theoretical considerations", in *African Social Research* (Manchester University Press), Dec. 1968, pp. 463-486.

—. 1974. *Migrating to urban centers of unemployment in tropical Africa*. Paper presented at the Eighth World Congress of Sociology, Toronto, Canada.

Gupta, K. L. 1970. "Personal saving in developing nations: further evidence", in *The Economic Record* (Economic Society of Australia and New Zealand), June 1970, pp. 243-249.

Gutkind, P. C. W. 1969. "Tradition, migration, urbanization, modernity and unemployment in Africa: the roots of instability", in *Canadian Journal of African Studies* (Montreal), Summer 1969, pp. 343-366.

Hamilton, C. H. 1956. "Population pressure and other factors affecting new rural-urban migration", in O. D. Duncan and J. J. Spengler (eds.): *Demographic analysis*. Glencoe, Ill., The Free Press.

—. 1975. "A note on surplus labour and risk aversion", in *Journal of Development Economics*, June 1975, pp. 161-163.

Hance, W. A. 1970. *Population, migration and urbanization in Africa*. New York, Columbia University Press.

Harris, J. 1976. *Memorandum — Indonesian migration task force*. Paper presented at the World Bank Research Workshop on Rural-Urban Labor Market Interactions, Washington, DC.

—; Rempel, H. 1976. *Rural-urban labor migration and urban unemployment in Kenya* (draft). Cambridge, Mass., Massachusetts Institute of Technology.

—; Sabot, R. 1976. *Urban unemployment in LDCs: towards a more general search model*. Paper presented at the World Bank Research Workshop on Rural-Urban Labor Market Interactions, Washington, DC.

—; Todaro, M. P. 1970. "Migration, unemployment and development: a two-sector analysis", in *The American Economic Review*, Mar. 1970, pp. 126-142.

Harris, R. N. S.; Steer, E. F. 1968. "Demographic-resource push in rural migration: a Jamaican case study", in *Social and Economic Studies* (Kingston, Jamaica), Dec. 1968, pp. 398-406.

Bibliography

Hart, J. K. 1974. "Migration and the opportunity structure: a Ghanaian case study", in S. Amin (ed.): *Modern migrations in western Africa*. London, Oxford University Press.

Harvey, M. 1968. "Implications of migration to Freetown: a study of the relationship between migrants, housing and occupation", in *Civilisations* (Brussels, International Institute of Differing Civilizations), No. 2, pp. 247-269.

Hathaway, D. E. 1964. "Migration from agriculture: the historical record and its meaning", in C. Eicher and L. Witt (eds.): *Agriculture in economic development*. New York, McGraw-Hill.

Hay, M. J. 1974. *An economic analysis of rural-urban migration in Tunisia*. Minneapolis, Minn., University of Minnesota. Unpublished Ph.D. dissertation.

Herrick, B. H. 1965. *Urban migration and economic development in Chile*. Cambridge, Mass., and London, Massachusetts Institute of Technology Press.

—. 1971. "Urbanization and urban migration in Latin America: an economist's view", in F. Rabinovitz and F. Trueblood (eds.): *Latin American urban research*, Vol. 1. Beverly Hills, Calif., Sage Publications.

—. 1974. *Urban self-employment and changing expectations as influences on urban migration*. Cambridge, Mass., Massachusetts Institute of Technology. Mimeographed.

Hilton, T. E. 1966. "Depopulation and population movement in the upper region of Ghana", in *Bulletin of the Ghana Geography Association*, No. 1, pp. 27-47.

Hoopengardner, T. 1974. *Rural-urban migration in less developed countries: a dynamic view*. Ann Arbor, Mich., University of Michigan, Center for Research on Economic Development. Discussion paper no. 33.

Houghton, D. H. 1960. "Men of two worlds: some aspects of migratory labour in South Africa", in *The South African Journal of Economics* (Braamfontein, Economic Society of South Africa), Oct. 1960, pp. 177-190.

House, W. J.; Rempel, H. 1976. "Labour market pressures and wage determination in less developed countries: the case of Kenya", in *Economic Development and Cultural Change* (forthcoming).

Huntington, H. 1974. *An empirical study of ethnic linkages in Kenyan rural-urban migration*. Binghamton, NY, State University of New York. Unpublished Ph.D. dissertation.

Husain, I. et al. 1965. *Social characteristics of the people of Karachi*. Karachi, Pakistan Institute of Development Economics.

Hutchinson, B. 1963. "The migrant population of urban Brazil", in *America Latina* (Rio de Janeiro), No. 2, pp. 41-71.

Hutton, C. R. 1970. "Rates of labour migration", in J. Gugler (ed.): *Urban growth in sub-Saharan Africa*. Kampala, Makerere Institute of Social Research.

Imoagene, S. O. 1969. "Psycho-social factors in rural-urban migration", in *The Nigerian Journal of Economic and Social Studies*, Nov. 1969, pp. 375-386.

International Labour Office. 1960. *Why labour leaves the land*. Geneva. Studies and reports, New series, No. 59.

—. 1965. *Report to the Government of Thailand on internal migration*. Geneva. Doc. ILO/OTA/Thailand/R.26. Mimeographed.

—. 1969. *Employment policy in Africa: problems and policies*. Geneva. Report IV (1), Third African Regional Conference, Accra.

—. 1972. *Employment, incomes and equality: a strategy for increasing productive employment in Kenya*. Geneva.

—. 1974. *Labour force and world population growth*, special issue of *Bulletin of Labour Statistics* (Geneva).

International Planned Parenthood Federation. 1974. *People* (London), No. 4.

Jack, A. B. 1970. "A short-run model of inter-regional migration", in *The Manchester School of Economic and Social Studies* (University of Manchester, Department of Economics), Mar. 1970, pp. 15-28.

Jackson, J. A. (ed.). 1969. *Migration*. Cambridge University Press.

Johnson, G. 1971. "The structure of rural-urban migration models", in *East African Economic Review* (Nairobi), June 1971, pp. 21-28.

— ; Whitelaw, W. E. 1972. *Urban-rural income transfers in Kenya : an estimated remittance function*. University of Nairobi, Institute of Development Studies. Mimeographed.

Johnson, M. 1964. "Migrants' progress", in *Bulletin of the Ghana Geography Association*, No. 2, pp. 4-25.

—. 1965. "Migrants' progress, part II", in *Bulletin of the Ghana Geography Association*, No. 1, pp. 13-40.

Jolly, R. 1970. "Rural-urban migration : dimensions, causes, issues and policies", in R. Jolly (ed.) : *Education in Africa : research and action*. Nairobi, East African Publishing House.

— ; de Kadt, E. ; Singer, H. ; Wilson, F. 1973. *Third World employment : problems and strategy*. Harmondsworth, Mddx., Penguin Education.

Jones, D. W. 1974. *Migration and urban unemployment in dualistic economic development*. University of Chicago. Unpublished Ph.D. dissertation.

Joshi, H. ; Lubell, H. ; Mouly, J. 1976. *Abidjan : urban development and employment in the Ivory Coast*. Geneva, ILO.

Jurgen, H. W. ; Tracey, K. A. A. ; Mitchell, P. K. 1966. "Internal migration in Liberia", in *The Bulletin — The Journal of the Sierra Leone Geographic Association*, No. 10, pp. 39-59.

Keely, C. 1975. *Demographic and legal changes in US immigration*. Paper presented at the Conference on International Migration from the Philippines. East-West Center.

Kilby, P. 1967. "Industrial relations and wage determination : failure of the Anglo-Saxon model", in *The Journal of Developing Areas*, No. 4, pp. 489-520.

Knight, J. B. 1972. "Rural-urban income comparisons and migration in Ghana", in *Bulletin of the Oxford University Institute of Economics and Statistics* (Oxford, Blackwell), May 1972, pp. 199-228.

Knowles, J. C. ; Anker, R. 1975. *Economic determinants of demographic behaviour in Kenya*. Geneva, ILO. World Employment Programme paper for restricted distribution only. Mimeographed.

Kuper, H. (ed.). 1965. *Urbanization and migration in west Africa*. Berkeley, University of California Press.

Kuroda, T. 1965. *Internal migration : an overview of problems and studies*. Paper presented at the United Nations World Population Conference, Belgrade, Yugoslavia.

Kuznets, S. 1964. "Introduction : population redistribution, migration and economic growth", in H. T. Eldridge and D. S. Thomas (eds.) : *Population redistribution and economic growth, United States, 1870-1950*, Vol. III. Philadelphia, American Philosophical Association.

Bibliography

—. 1971. *Economic growth of nations.* Cambridge, Mass., Harvard University Press.

—. 1974. *Fertility differentials between less developed and developed regions: components and implications.* New Haven, Conn., Yale University, Economic Growth Center. Discussion paper no. 217.

Laber, G. 1972. "Lagged response in the decision to migrate: a comment", in *Journal of Regional Science*, Aug. 1972, pp. 307-310.

Lakdawala, D. T. et al. 1963. *Work, wages and well-being in the Indian metropolis: economic survey of Bombay City.* University of Bombay.

Lal, D. 1976. *On the measurement of rural-urban income differentials: comments.* Paper presented at the World Bank Research Workshop on Rural-Urban Labor Market Interactions, Washington, DC.

Land, K. 1969. "Duration of residence and prospective migration: further evidence", in *Demography*, No. 2, pp. 133-140.

Lansing, J. B.; Mueller, E. (eds.). 1967. *The geographic mobility of labor.* Ann Arbor, Mich., University of Michigan, Institute for Social Research, Survey Research Center.

Lee, E. S. 1966. "A theory of migration", in *Demography*, No. 1, pp. 47-57.

Lee, M. *The facts behind Seoul's exploding population.* Seoul National University. Unpublished.

Levi, J. F. S. 1971. "Migration and unemployment in Sierra Leone", in *Manpower and Unemployment Research in Africa: a Newsletter* (Montreal, McGill University, Center for Developing Area Studies), No. 2, pp. 20-25.

Levy, M.; Wadycki, W. 1972a. "A comparison of young and middle-aged migration in Venezuela", in *Annals of Regional Science*, No. 2, pp. 73-85.

—; —. 1972b. "Lifetime versus one-year migration in Venezuela", in *Journal of Regional Science*, Dec. 1972, pp. 407-415.

—; —. 1973. "The influence of family and friends on geographic labor mobility: an international comparison", in *The Review of Economics and Statistics*, May 1973, pp. 198-203.

—; —. 1974a. "Education and the decision to migrate: an econometric analysis of migration in Venezuela", in *Econometrica* (New Haven, Conn., Econometric Society), Mar. 1974, pp. 377-388.

—; —. 1974b. "What is the opportunity cost of moving? Reconsideration of the effects of distance on migration", in *Economic Development and Cultural Change*, Jan. 1974, pp. 198-214.

Lewis, W. A. 1954. "Economic development with unlimited supplies of labour", in *The Manchester School of Economic and Social Studies*, May 1954, pp. 139-191.

—. 1970. "Summary: the causes of unemployment in less developed countries and some research topics", in *International Labour Review*, May 1970, pp. 547-554.

Leys, C. 1973. "Interpreting African underdevelopment: reflections on the ILO report on employment, incomes and equality in Kenya", in *African Affairs* (London, Royal African Society), Oct. 1973, pp. 419-429.

Lipton, M. 1976. *Migration from rural areas of poor countries: the impact on rural productivity and income distribution.* Paper presented at the World Bank Research Workshop on Rural-Urban Labor Market Interactions, Washington, DC.

Little, L. 1965. *West African urbanization: a study of voluntary associations in social change.* Cambridge University Press.

Lopes, J. R. B. 1961. "Aspects of the adjustment of rural migrants to urban-industrial conditions in São Paulo, Brazil", in P. Hauser (ed.) : *Urbanization in Latin America*. Paris, UNESCO.

Lubell, H. 1974. *Urbanisation and employment : insights from a series of case studies of Third World metropolitan cities*. Geneva, ILO. World Employment Programme paper for restricted distribution only. Mimeographed.

Mabogunje, A. 1970. "Migration policy and regional development in Nigeria", in *The Nigerian Journal of Economic and Social Studies*, No. 2, pp. 243-262.

Mabro, R. 1967. "Industrial growth, agricultural underemployment and the Lewis model : the Egyptian case, 1937 to 1965", in *Journal of Development Studies*, July 1967, pp. 322-351.

MacDonald, L. D. ; MacDonald, J. S. 1968. "Motives and objectives of migration : selective migration and preferences toward rural and urban life", in *Social and Economic Studies*, Dec. 1968, pp. 417-434.

McDonald, S. L. 1971. *Economic factors in farm outmigration : a survey and evaluation of the literature*. Austin, Tex., University of Texas, Department of Economics. Mimeographed.

McQueen, A. J. 1969. "Unemployment and future orientation of Nigerian school-leavers", in *Canadian Journal of African Studies* (Montreal), Summer 1969, pp. 441-462.

Maddox, J. G. 1960. "Private and social costs of the movement of people out of agriculture", in *The American Economic Review*, No. 2, pp. 392-402.

Mahalingam, N. 1964. "India's population problem and internal migration", in *Population Review*, July 1964, pp. 45-49.

Mangin, W. 1967. "Latin American squatter settlements : a problem and a solution", in *Latin American Research Review*, Summer 1967, pp. 65-98.

Mar, J. M. 1961. "Migration and urbanization", in P. Hauser (ed.) : *Urbanization in Latin America*. Paris, UNESCO.

Meier, G. M. 1976 (3rd. ed.). *Leading issues in development economics*. London and New York, Oxford University Press.

Merrick, T. ; Brito, F. A. 1974. *Study of the labor market in a rapidly growing urban area*. Washington, DC, World Bank. Summary report.

Miller, E. M. 1973. "Is out-migration affected by economic conditions ?", in *Southern Economic Journal* (Chapel Hill, NC, Southern Economic Association), Jan. 1973, pp. 396-405.

Mincer, J. 1974. *Schooling, experience, and earnings*. New York, National Bureau of Economic Research/Columbia University Press.

Miracle, M. P. ; Berry, S. S. 1970. "Migrant labour and economic development", in *Oxford Economic Papers*, Mar. 1970, pp. 86-108.

Mitchell, J. C. 1959. "The causes of labour migration", in *Bulletin of the Inter-African Labour Institute* (London, Commission for Technical Co-operation in Africa south of the Sahara), Jan. 1959, pp. 12-47.

Morawetz, D. 1974. "Employment implications of industrialisation in developing countries: a survey", in *The Economic Journal* (London, Macmillan), Sep. 1974, pp. 491-542.

Morrill, R. L. 1965. *Migration and the spread and growth of urban settlement*. Lund (Sweden), Gleerup. Lund studies in geography, Series B, No. 26.

— ; Pitts, F. R. 1967. "Marriage, migration and the mean information field : a study in uniqueness and generality", in *Annals of the Association of American Geographers* (Washington, DC), Vol. 57.

Morrison, P. 1967. "Duration of residence and prospective migration: the evaluation of a stochastic model", in *Demography*, No. 2, pp. 553-561.

—. 1973. *Migration from distressed areas: its meaning for regional policy*. Santa Monica, Calif., RAND memorandum R-1103-EDA/FF/NIH.

Muth, R. F. 1971. "Migration: chicken or egg?", in *Southern Economic Journal*, Jan. 1971, pp. 295-306.

Myers, G. C. 1967. "Migration and modernization: the case of Puerto Rico, 1950-1960", in *Social and Economic Studies*, Dec. 1967, pp. 425-431.

Nabila, J. 1974. *Migration of the Fra Fra in northern Ghana: a case study of cyclical labour migration in west Africa*. East Lansing, Mich., Michigan State University. Unpublished Ph.D. dissertation.

Nelson, J. 1969. *Migrants, urban poverty, and instability in developing nations*. Cambridge, Mass., Harvard University, Center for International Affairs. Occasional paper no. 22.

—. 1974. *Sojourners vs. new urbanites: causes and consequences of temporary vs. permanent cityward migration in developing countries*. Cambridge, Mass., Harvard University.

—. 1975. *Politics and the urban poor in modernizing nations* (draft; mimeographed).

Ng, R. 1970. "A study of recent internal migration in Thailand", in *Journal of Tropical Geography* (University of Malaya and University of Singapore), Vol. 31, pp. 65-78.

Oberai, A. S. 1975. *An analysis of migration to Greater Khartoum (Sudan)*. Geneva, ILO. World Employment Programme paper for restricted distribution only. Mimeographed.

Okun, B.; Richardson, R. W. 1961. "Regional income inequality and internal population migration", in *Economic Development and Cultural Change*, Jan. 1961, pp. 128-143.

Ominde, S. H. 1965. "Population movements to the main urban areas of Kenya", in *Cahiers d'Etudes Africaines* (Paris, Ecole Pratique des Hautes Etudes), No. 4, pp. 593-617.

—. 1968. "Internal migration of the economically active age group in Kenya", in H. Berger (ed.): *Ost-Afrikanische Studien*. Erlangen-Nürnberg, Friedrich Alexander Universität, Wirtschaft und Sozialgeographischen Institut.

Organization of American States, Inter-American Committee on the Alliance for Progress (CIAP). 1969. *Urbanization in metropolitan Lima-Callão*. Doc. OEA/Ser.H/XIV, CIAP/365 (English).

Panofsky, H. E. 1960. "Migrant labour in Africa south of the Sahara: the significance of labour migration for the economic welfare of Ghana and the Voltaic Republic", in *Bulletin of the Inter-African Labour Institute* (Brazzaville), July 1960, pp. 30-45.

—. 1963. "Migratory labour in Africa: a bibliographical note", in *The Journal of Modern African Studies* (Cambridge University Press), No. 4, pp. 521-529.

Pastore, J. 1968. *Satisfaction among migrants to Brasilia, Brazil: a sociological interpretation*. Madison, Wis., University of Wisconsin. Unpublished Ph.D. dissertation.

Perlman, J. 1971. *The fate of migrants in Rio's favelas: the myth of marginality*. Cambridge, Mass., Massachusetts Institute of Technology. Unpublished Ph.D. dissertation.

Piault, M. P. 1961. "Migrant labour in Africa south of the Sahara: the migration of workers in west Africa", in *Bulletin of the Inter-African Labour Institute*, Feb. 1961, pp. 98-110.

Planungsgruppe Ritter. 1974. *Report on two surveys*. Geneva, ILO. World Employment Programme paper for restricted distribution only. Mimeographed.

Pokrant, R. J. 1966. "Labor migration and urbanization: a research proposal", in *African Urban Notes*, No. 1, pp. 15-18.

Porter, R. C. 1973. *Labor migration and urban unemployment in less developed countries: comment*. Ann Arbor, Mich., University of Michigan. Discussion paper no. 29.

Prothero, R. M. 1967. "Characteristics of rural-urban migration and the effects of their movements upon the composition of population in rural and urban areas in sub-Saharan Africa", in *Proceedings of the World Population Conference, Belgrade, 1965*, Vol. IV. New York, United Nations. Sales No.: E.66.XIII.8.

Ranis, G. 1962. "Investment criteria, productivity and economic development", in *Quarterly Journal of Economics*, May 1962.

Rao, V. K. R. V.; Desai, P. B. 1965. *Greater Delhi: a study in urbanization, 1940-57*. Bombay, Asia Publishing House.

Ravenstein, E. G. 1885. "The laws of migration", in *Journal of the Royal Statistical Society* (London), June 1885, pp. 167-227.

—. 1889. "The laws of migration", in *Journal of the Royal Statistical Society*, June 1889, pp. 241-301.

Rempel, H. 1971a. *Labor migration into urban centers and urban unemployment in Kenya*. Madison, Wis., University of Wisconsin. Unpublished Ph.D. dissertation.

—. 1971b. "The rural to urban migrant in Kenya", in *African Urban Notes*, No. 1, pp. 53-72.

Repetto, R. 1974. *The interaction of fertility and the size distribution of income*. Cambridge, Mass., Harvard University, Center for Population Studies. Research paper no. 8.

Rich, W. 1973. *Smaller families through social and economic progress*. Washington, DC, Overseas Development Council.

Ridker, R. G.; Nordberg, O. S. 1976. *Labour policy and fertility in developing countries*. Geneva, ILO. World Employment Programme paper for restricted distribution only. Mimeographed.

Roussel, L. 1970. "Measuring rural-urban drift in developing countries: a suggested method", in *International Labour Review*, Mar. 1970, pp. 229-246.

Rostow, W. W. 1960. *The stages of economic growth*. Cambridge University Press.

Sabolo, Y. 1975. "Employment and unemployment, 1960-90", in *International Labour Review*, Dec. 1975, pp. 401-417.

Sabot, R. H. 1975a. *Economic development, structural change and urban migration*. Oxford, The Clarendon Press.

—. 1975b. *The meaning and measurement of urban surplus labor*. Washington, DC, World Bank. Mimeographed.

— (with Barnum, H.). 1976. *Migration, education and urban surplus labour*. Paris, OECD Development Centre.

—. 1975d. *Research proposal: a comparative analysis of rural-urban labor market interactions*. Washington, DC, World Bank. Mimeographed.

Sahota, G. S. 1968. "An economic analysis of internal migration in Brazil", in *Journal of Political Economy*, Mar./Apr. 1968, pp. 218-245.

Sakdejayonto, Y. 1973. *Village life near Bangkok*. Kyoto University, Center for Southeast Asian Studies.

Savla, C. 1973. *Some aspects of out-migration from Gujerat (with special reference to Kutch district)*. University of Bombay. Unpublished Ph.D. dissertation.

Schaefer, K. (assisted by Spindel, C. R.). 1976. *São Paulo: urban development and employment*. Geneva, ILO.

Schuh, G. E. 1976. *Out-migration, rural productivity and the distribution of income*. Paper presented at the World Bank Research Workshop on Rural-Urban Labor Market Interactions, Washington, DC.

Schultz, T. P. 1969. *Population growth and internal migration in Colombia*. Santa Monica, Calif., The Rand Corporation.

—. 1971. "Rural-urban migration in Colombia", in *The Review of Economics and Statistics*, May 1971, pp. 157-163.

—. 1975. *The determinants of internal migration in Venezuela: an application of the polytomous logistic model*. Paper presented at the World Congress of the Econometric Society, Toronto.

—. 1976. *Notes on the estimation of migration decision functions*. Paper presented at the World Bank Research Workshop on Rural-Urban Labor Market Interactions, Washington, DC.

Schwartz, A. 1973. "Interpreting the effect of distance on migration", in *Journal of Political Economy*, Sep./Oct. 1973, pp. 1153-1169.

Sen, A. K. 1966. "Peasants and dualism with or without surplus labour", in *Journal of Political Economy*, Oct. 1966, pp. 425-450.

Senior, C. 1962. "Migration as a process and migrant as a person", in *Population Review*, Jan. 1962, pp. 30-41.

Shryock, H. S. 1969. *Survey statistics on reasons for moving*. Paper presented at the General Conference of the International Union for the Scientific Study of Population, London.

Silvers, A.; de Mello Moreira, M. 1973. "A absorção da força de trabalho nãoqualificada em Minas Gerais: Evidência em favor da hipótese de Todaro?" Paper presented at the First Annual Meeting of the Associação Nacional de Centros de Pos-Graduação em Economia, Secretaria Executiva: CEDEPLAR/URMG.

Simmons, A. 1970. *The emergence of planning orientations in a modernizing community: migration, adaptation, and family planning in highland Colombia*. Ithaca, NY, Cornell University, Latin American Studies Programme. Dissertation series, No. 15.

Singh, S. K. 1970. *Rural-urban wage differential*. Washington, DC, World Bank, Basic Research Center. Working paper no. 70-14.

Sjaastad, L. A. 1962. "The costs and returns of human migration", in *Journal of Political Economy*, Oct. 1962, Part 2, pp. 80-93.

Skinner, E. P. 1965. "Labor migration among the Mossi of Upper Volta", in H. Kuper (ed.): *Urbanization and migration in west Africa*. Berkeley, Calif., University of California Press.

Smith, P. 1975. *A demographic overview of out-migration from the Philippines*. East-West Population Institute, Conference on International Migration from the Philippines.

Southall, A. W. 1968. "The pattern of migration in Madagascar and its theoretical implications", in *African Urban Notes*, No. 1, pp. 14-22.

Spengler, J. J. 1969. "Population movements and problems in sub-Saharan Africa", in E. A. G. Robinson (ed.) : *Economic development for Africa south of the Sahara*. London, Macmillan.

Steel, W. F. ; Takagi, Y. 1976. *The intermediate sector, unemployment, and the employment-output conflict*. Nashville, Tenn., Vanderbilt University, Department of Economics. Mimeographed.

Stiglitz, J. E. 1969. "Rural-urban migration, surplus labour, and the relationship between urban and rural wages", in *Eastern Africa Economic Review*, Dec. 1969, pp. 1-27.

—. 1974. "Alternative theories of wage determination and unemployment in LDCs : the labor turnover model", in *Quarterly Journal of Economics*, May 1974, pp. 194-227.

—. 1976. *The structure of labor markets and shadow prices in LDCs*. Paper presented at the World Bank Research Workshop on Rural-Urban Labor Market Interactions, Washington, DC.

Stolnitz, G. J. 1974. "Population and labor force in less developed regions : some main facts, theory and research needs", in E. O. Edwards (ed.) : *Employment in developing nations*. New York, Columbia University Press.

Stuart, R. C. ; Gregory, P. R. 1974. *A model of Soviet rural-urban migration*. Austin, Tex., University of Texas. Mimeographed.

Taber, S. R. 1968. *Economic opportunity and urban orientation as factors in Uganda migration*. Paper presented at the University Social Sciences Council Conference, University of East Africa, Makerere University College, Kampala.

Tachi, M. 1964. "Regional income disparity and internal migration of population in Japan", in *Economic Development and Cultural Change*, Jan. 1964, pp. 186-204.

Thomas, B. 1954. *Migration and economic growth : a study of Great Britain and the Atlantic economy*. Cambridge University Press.

Thomas, R. 1970. *Internal migration in Latin America : analysis of recent literature*. Paper presented at the National Conference for Latin Americanist Geographers, Ball State University, Muncie, Ind.

Thomlinson, R. 1962. "Methodological needs in migration research", in *Population Review*, Jan. 1962, pp. 59-64.

Thormann, P. H. 1970. "The rural-urban income differential and minimum wage fixing criteria", in *International Labour Review*, Aug. 1970, pp. 127-147.

Todaro, M. P. 1968. "The urban employment problem in less developed countries: an analysis of demand and supply", in *Yale Economic Essays* (New Haven, Conn., Yale University), Fall 1968, pp. 329-402.

—. 1969. "A model of labor migration and urban unemployment in less developed countries", in *The American Economic Review*, Mar. 1969, pp. 138-148.

—. 1971a. *Education and rural-urban migration : theoretical constructs and empirical evidence from Kenya*. Paper presented at the Conference on Urban Unemployment in Africa, Institute for Development Studies, University of Sussex, Brighton.

—. 1971b. "Income expectations, rural-urban migration and employment in Africa", in *International Labour Review*, Nov. 1971, pp. 387-413.

Bibliography

—. 1972. "Reply to comment on labour migration in less developed countries", in *Manpower and unemployment research in Africa*, No. 2, pp. 49-51.

—. 1976a. "Rural-urban migration, unemployment and job probabilities: recent theoretical and empirical research", in Ansley J. Coale (ed.): *Economic factors in population growth*. London, Macmillan.

—. 1976b. "Urban job expansion, induced migration and rising unemployment: a formulation and simplified empirical test for LDCs", in *Journal of Development Economics* (forthcoming).

Toosie, M.; Scully, G. W. 1976. *Interim report on sample household survey on economic conditions in Tehran and migration to Tehran*. Paper presented at the World Bank Research Workshop on Rural-Urban Labor Market Interactions, Washington, DC.

Trebous, M. 1970. *Migration and development: the case of Algeria*. Paris, OECD Development Centre.

Turner, H. A. 1970. "Wage planning, growth and employment in less developed countries", abstract in *International Labour Review*, May 1970, pp. 542-543.

Turnham, D. (assisted by Jaeger, I.). 1971. *The employment problem in less developed countries: a review of evidence*. Paris, OECD Development Centre.

Udall, A. 1973. *Migration and employment in Bogotá, Colombia*. New Haven, Conn., Yale University. Unpublished Ph.D. dissertation.

United Nations. 1967. *Proceedings of the World Population Conference, Belgrade, 1965*, Vol. IV: *Migration, urbanization, economic development*. New York. Sales No.: E.66.XIII.8.

—. 1974. *Statistical yearbook 1973*. New York. Sales No.: E/F.74.XVII.1.

—, Department of Economic and Social Affairs. 1970. *Methods of measuring internal migration*. New York. Population studies, No. 47. Sales No.: E.70.XIII.3.

Vanderkamp, J. 1971. "Migration flows, their determinants and the effects of return migration", in *Journal of Political Economy*, Sep./Oct. 1971, pp. 1012-1031.

Van Velsen, J. 1960. "Labor migration as a positive factor in the continuity of Tonga tribal society", in *Economic Development and Cultural Change*, Apr. 1960, pp. 265-278.

Vogel, W. M. 1968. *Is labor migration of decreasing significance in the economy of east Africa?* Syracuse, NY, Syracuse University, Program of East African Studies.

Warriner, D. 1970. "Problems of rural-urban migration: some suggestions for investigation", in *International Labour Review*, May 1970, pp. 441-451.

Webb, R. 1973. *Income and employment in the urban traditional sector in Peru*. Princeton, NJ, Princeton University, Department of Economics. Mimeographed.

Wertheimer, R. F. 1970. *The monetary rewards of migration within the United States*. Washington, DC, The Urban Institute.

Wéry, R.; Rodgers, G. B. and Hopkins, M. D. 1974. *BACHUE-2: Version-I: a population and employment model for the Philippines*. Geneva, ILO. World Employment Programme paper for restricted distribution only. Mimeographed.

Wilkening, E. A. 1968. *Comparison of migrants in two rural and one urban area of central Brazil*. Madison, Wis., University of Wisconsin, Land Tenure Center.

Yap, L. 1972. *Internal migration and economic development in Brazil.* Cambridge, Mass., Harvard University. Unpublished Ph.D. dissertation.

—. 1975. *Internal migration in less developed countries: a survey of the literature.* Washington, DC, World Bank. Urban Poverty Task Force paper.

Zachariah, K. C. 1964. *Migrants in Greater Bombay* (preliminary version). Chembur, Bombay, Demographic Training and Research Centre.

—. 1966. "Bombay migration study: a pilot analysis of migration to an Asian metropolis", in *Demography*, No. 2, pp. 378-392. Reprinted in G. Breeze (ed.): *The city in newly developing countries.* Englewood Cliffs, NJ, Prentice-Hall.

Zarembka, P. 1972. *Towards a theory of economic development.* San Francisco, Holden-Day.